Dear Jaden

Christmas 2013

CASE
FOR
CHRIST
FOR KIDS

love
Uncle Rob & Aunt Deb

D. Cousins

CASE
FOR
CHRIST
FOR KIDS

LEE STROBEL
WITH JESSE FLOREA

ZONDERkidz

ZONDERKIDZ

Case for Christ 90-Day Devotional
Copyright © 2013 by Lee Strobel

This title is also available as a Zondervan ebook. Visit www.zondervan.com/ebooks.

Requests for information should be addressed to:

Zonderkidz, 5300 Patterson Ave SE, Grand Rapids, Michigan 49530

ISBN 978-0-310-73392-8

Cover design: Deborah Washburn
Coverphoto: Shutterstock
Interior design: Matthew Van Zomeren and Ben Fetterley

Printed in the United States of America

13 14 15 16 17 18 19 20 /DCI/ 20 19 18 17 16 15 14 13 12 11 10 9 8 7 6 5 4 3 2 1

CONTENTS

FOREWORD

You might look at this book and wonder, *Why does there need to be a case for Christ? Just look at creation. Look at all the great Christians who've done amazing things in his name. Look at the lives he's changed. Isn't it obvious that Jesus existed and has great power?*

You might be growing up in a Christian home where studying the Bible is the norm. I didn't. Instead of embracing the good news about Jesus Christ, I didn't want anything to do with God. I was an open-minded atheist and proud of it. I thought religious people needed a crutch, and I enjoyed making fun of their faith. As you go through life, you'll probably meet a lot of people who are like the person I was.

So what changed? Well, my life hit a wall. It might have looked good from the outside. I had graduated from Yale Law School, one of the most prestigious in the world, and was legal editor of the *Chicago Tribune*. Professionally, I was at the top of my game. I lived in an exciting, upscale neighborhood. Personally, however, I was struggling. After a period of searching, my wife, Leslie, had decided to become a follower of Jesus Christ. To me, this was awful news! How could she believe in a God who so obviously didn't exist? Quickly, I became sarcastic toward her newfound faith. I'd ridicule her when she tried to explain Christianity to me. I even thought about leaving my marriage and my two beautiful children.

Before it was too late, I began noticing powerful changes in Leslie. Attractive changes. I decided to honestly investigate Christianity. I assumed I'd easily be able to prove my wife and her faith wrong. Using the tools I learned in law school and as a journalist, I studied Christianity. I read about the early disciples, researched the history of Jesus, and sought out credible sources. Do you know what I found? My wife—and billions of people before her—were right. God exists. Jesus really died for my sins and rose from the dead.

That's when Jesus did a miracle. No, he didn't make me blind and restore my sight or heal me from a fatal disease. But he changed my life. Once I prayed to accept Jesus as my Savior, my life changed for the better. My marriage became stronger than it ever was before. I was a better father to my children. Then I wrote a book about my quest for the truth of Christianity. I called it *The Case for Christ: A Journalist's Personal Investigation of the Evidence for Jesus*. That book has sold millions of copies and been translated into dozens of languages. Maybe you'll read it someday.

But for now, I hope you will investigate these devotionals for the next ninety days. I didn't build a foundation on Christ when I was your age—and I nearly paid a huge price. By knowing what you believe and why you've put your trust in Jesus, you can stand strong in your faith and avoid mistakes I made. Plus, if you ever meet somebody—like I was—who wants to poke holes in your beliefs, you'll "be prepared to give an answer to everyone who asks you to give the reason for the hope that you have. But do this with gentleness and respect" (1 Peter 3:15).

FOREWORD

It's my prayer that as you read these truths—truths about who Jesus is, what he has done, how he wants you to live, why you should try to grow closer to him, how he fits into God's triune nature, and how the Bible was put together—they will help you build your own case for Christ. And it'll be a case that you will stake your life on.

—*Lee Strobel*

DISCOVER THE REAL JESUS

There is no Christianity without Christ. But Jesus didn't come to earth to start a new religion. He came to rebuild the relationship between people and God. Jesus lived, died, and rose from the dead so we could know God personally.

Our purpose in life isn't to follow a bunch of religious rules. We're called to follow Jesus. And to follow him, we must know him.

As you read through this book, you learn more about Jesus' life. You'll discover the Jesus of history. You'll hear Jesus the teacher. You'll see Jesus the miracle worker. And you'll come face-to-face with Jesus the risen Lord. But the best way to find the real Jesus is to read about him in the Gospels. Matthew, Mark, Luke, and John carefully and accurately wrote about Jesus' life. In a couple of weeks, you'll come to a story in this book titled "Reality Check." At the end of it, you'll be asked to commit to read one of the Gospels. But before you even begin this book, we want to challenge you to read *all* of the Gospels.

In order to get to know Christ—*really* know Christ—the best place to start is in the Gospels. This book contains ninety devotions. There are eighty-nine chapters in the

Gospels (Matthew is the longest with twenty-eight, while Mark has just sixteen). So if you read just one devotion and one chapter of the Bible each day, you'll be able to complete this book and all of the Gospels in less than three months! Are you up to the challenge?

You may have to put in a little extra time and effort now, but you'll reap rewards right away and into the future. Nothing is more important than knowing Christ. We created this book to help you on that journey. Take time each day to dig into your faith in the "Examine the Case" section. Look up the Scripture passage in the "Final Word." If you make the effort to get really involved in the content of this book and the Bible, you'll be amazed by all you discover about Christ.

HOT DOG FAITH

Who doesn't love hot dogs? Sure, some people shy away from this frankly popular frank. But most Americans love to eat hot dogs—lots of them.

During just the Fourth of July holiday, Americans consume 150 million frankfurters! If you put that many hot dogs in a line, they would stretch around the world from New York City to Sydney, Australia.

But have you ever looked at the ingredients in an inexpensive hot dog? The first ingredient is almost always mechanically separated turkey or chicken. But what is that? According to the U.S. Department of Agriculture (USDA), it's a "paste-like and batter-like poultry product produced by forcing bones, with attached edible tissue, through a sieve or similar device under high pressure." *Yum.* Most hot dogs contain pork, which the USDA says can be any "meat" removed from the bone by "advanced meat recovery machinery." Other ingredients include water, corn syrup, beef, salt, sodium phosphate, sodium erythorbate, sodium nitrate, and maltodextrin.

Does your mouth water thinking of those ingredients? Probably not.

EXAMINE THE CASE

Sadly, for the last fifty years, people have been building their religious beliefs like a cheap hot dog. Instead of following God's Word and traditional Christianity, they fuse together their own beliefs by grabbing a little of this philosophy, a bit of another idea, and a smidgen of some other outlook and jamming them all together. Maybe you know somebody who says he believes in God, but doesn't believe in hell and thinks we should do whatever makes us feel best.

That can look good on the outside—sort of like a hot dog—but inside it's a pasty, bland, and non-nutritious belief system. God wants us to be strong. He gave us the Bible so that we could know what to believe and how to live for him. Yet many people pick and choose which parts they want to believe. Then they mix in harmful additives from other religions.

That's not healthy (sort of like eating a cheap hot dog). When you eat the pure meat of God's Word, you grow strong in your faith. The writer of Hebrews says, "Solid food is for the mature, who by constant use have trained themselves to distinguish good from evil." By reading your Bible and listening to godly teachers, you feed yourself good meat ... not some strange, harmful mystery meat.

FINAL WORD

"Solid food is for the mature, who by constant use have trained themselves to distinguish good from evil" *Hebrews 5:14*.

DIG IN

Jeremy Jangle Michael McBoom
Simply refused to clean his room.
He tried to obey and wasn't unkind.
He just was afraid of what he might find.
The door didn't budge. The floor was all gone.
He thought about cleaning, but not for too long.
His socks mounded up like a pile of hay.
The stench was so bad that his dog ran away.
There were sweaty T-shirts, jackets with stains,
Empty Coke bottles and old candy canes.
Homework assignments that were long overdue
Hid under a book and some Dinty Moore stew.
Dishes were piled with gross crusts of bread.
His hamster was lost and presumably dead.
Jeremy's mom had at last seen enough.
She went to his door and said with a huff,
"Your room is atrocious. It's time to begin.
Go grab a shovel. You have to dig in."

EXAMINE THE CASE

Jeremy was afraid to clean his room because he didn't know what he might discover. But when you dig into the Bible, you can be confident of what you'll find: the truth.

God's Word is active, alive, and powerful. Daniel B. Wallace traveled the world to study ancient biblical manuscripts. He taught at Dallas Theological Seminary and is considered one of the world's best authorities on God's Word. Wallace said, "The Bible deserves to be rigorously investigated because the Bible claims to be a historical document. We have to ask the Bible tough questions because that's what Christ not only invites us to do, but requires of us to do."

Don't be afraid to dig into the Bible. For centuries archaeologists in the Holy Land have dug up relics and other evidence that support the Bible. Not only is God's Word historically accurate, it truthfully tells us about God's character and how he wants us to live.

The next time you pick up your Bible, follow Wallace's advice and act like the Bereans. The book of Acts says these people "studied the Scriptures carefully every day." Carefully study the Bible yourself to discover what it has to say. The more you dig in, the more you'll understand its truth.

FINAL WORD

"The Bereans were very glad to receive Paul's message. They studied the Scriptures carefully every day. They wanted to see if what Paul said was true" *Acts 17:11 NIRV*.

GET THE MESSAGE?

Cna yuo raed tihs? God gvae yuo an azmaing mnid. Jsut a fwe wrods aer spllede corcrtoly, yet yuo cna aulaclty uesdnatnrd waht you aer rdanieg. Rchearch sohws yuor mnid cna unsrcamlbe jmubedl wrods, btu it maeks yuo raed muhc mroe slwoly. It hlpes to hvae teh frsit and lsat ltteers in the rghit pclae. The rset can be a taotl mses. Tihs is bcuseae the huamn mnid deos not raed ervey lteter by istlef, but the wrod as a wlohe. Azanmig, huh? And yuo awlyas tghuhot slpeling wsa ipmorantt!

Several years ago, an email circulated around the world with a similar mixed-up message. It said only 50 percent of people could read it. Scientists say the percentage is actually much higher, but reading and understanding a jumbled message takes a lot longer than reading a normal message.

EXAMINE THE CASE

God gave you a brain that craves understanding. That's why people are so good at solving math problems and mysteries. We want to get at the truth, and God has given us the ability to do it.

Textual critics are experts who get at the truth of God's Word. Sometimes they have only a fragment of biblical manuscript (maybe a sentence or two) to study. Other times they have a whole book. They work hard to make sure every word in the Bible is correct, as they seek to determine the writer's original message. Bible expert Daniel B. Wallace says, "The quantity and quality of the New Testament manuscripts are unequalled in the ancient Greco-Roman world."

Wallace points out that for many ancient Greek authors, fewer than twenty copies of their writings exist. But the New Testament has more than 5,800 of the earliest Greek copies in existence—in fact, about 24,000 manuscripts in all. To get a better picture of what this means, if you stacked up copies of all the works of the average Greek author, the pile would be about four feet tall. But if you stacked up ancient copies of the New Testament, it would reach more than a mile high!

God wants you to know his message. He left a lot of evidence so we'd believe in his miracles and mighty power. And he trusted specific people with his words so they wouldn't get mixed up. The Bible is more than a history book. It's good for you. It nourishes you (Deuteronomy 8:3). It makes you stronger. Adn wehn yuo raed it, taht mesasge is claer.

FINAL WORD

"Man does not live on bread alone but on every word that comes from the mouth of the Lord" *Deuteronomy 8:3.*

LIKE A MAN ON THE MOON

An estimated 600 million people watched TV as U.S. astronauts Neil Armstrong and Buzz Aldrin landed on the moon on July 20, 1969. Several hours after hitting the surface, Aldrin celebrated the Lord's Supper in the Apollo 11 lunar module and privately thanked God for keeping them safe. The next day Armstrong became the first man to walk on the moon when he famously said, "That's one small step for man, one giant leap for mankind."

Five years after NASA put men on the moon, an author self-published a book called *We Never Went to the Moon: America's Thirty Billion Dollar Swindle*. Since that time, other people have come up with theories stating that the moon landings were faked. Some said NASA worked with Walt Disney to stage the landings. Numerous documentaries have been made, saying the landings were a hoax. That would mean a lot of people were involved in the conspiracy. More than 400,000 people worked on the Apollo project over the course of ten years. And all of them have stood by the fact that men really walked on the moon. The only people being swindled are those who believe it was all a hoax.

EXAMINE THE CASE

Conspiracy theories are nothing new. Once the chief priests (who orchestrated Jesus' arrest and crucifixion) learned that Jesus had risen from the dead, they gave the soldiers money to say, "His disciples came during the night and stole him away while we were asleep" (Matthew 28:12–13). But the disciples and other people saw Jesus after he came out of the tomb. They knew he was alive. The disciples were willing to die rather than deny that Jesus had risen from the dead. Surely, if they had "stolen Jesus' body," they would've changed their stories to save themselves.

Theories about Jesus faking his death continue even today. People write books saying that Jesus wasn't God and didn't rise from the dead. Sadly, not everybody who hears about Jesus' resurrection believes. First Corinthians 1:18 says, "For the message of the cross is foolishness to those who are perishing, but to us who are being saved it is the power of God." God's power and victory over death were shown on the cross. While Jesus' resurrection may sound unbelievable—sort of like a man walking on the moon—it's something you can absolutely believe in.

FINAL WORD

"For the message of the cross is foolishness to those who are perishing, but to us who are being saved it is the power of God"
1 Corinthians 1:18.

HIS STORY
FROM HISTORY

Do you think Jesus ever hit his funny bone and had his hand go numb? Or if the Lord bumped his knee just right, did his foot involuntarily shoot into the air?

It's kind of weird to think about God's Son having normal human bodily responses. But the Bible clearly says that Jesus became flesh and dwelt among us (John 1:14). When he got tired, he slept. When he was hungry, his stomach rumbled. And if he ate too fast, he might have suffered from aerophagia—frequent belching after eating too quickly and swallowing a lot of air. (Can you imagine Jesus burping?) That may sound gross, but the fact is Jesus was 100 percent God and 100 percent human.

The Bible contains a number of verses that show Jesus' humanity. He got angry. He cried. He experienced pain.

When Jesus walked through the countryside teaching about God's kingdom, he probably got sweaty. (It's pretty hot and dusty in some parts of the Holy Land.) If it had been too long between baths, he might have even had BO (as in "body odor").

EXAMINE THE CASE

Because Jesus was fully human, he understands everything you're going through. He knows what it's like to grow up with siblings and have friends stab you in the back. But it's also important to remember that Jesus was a real person who lived during a real time in history.

The books of Matthew, Mark, Luke, and John are filled with stories about Jesus' life. But he also appears in numerous other historical writings. In the first century AD, a Jewish historian named Flavius Josephus documented that Jesus was a teacher who performed "surpassing feats" and had a group of disciples who continued to follow him after his death. Tacitus, a Roman historian and senator, wrote about Jesus' execution by Pontius Pilate. And Jesus is mentioned in other ancient writings as well.

As you put your faith in Jesus and build the foundation of your faith, you can be confident about who Jesus Christ really is. He's a real man who lived in a real place during a real time in history. And he's really God's Son who really loves you a lot, right now.

FINAL WORD

"The Word became flesh and made his dwelling among us. We have seen his glory, the glory of the one and only Son, who came from the Father, full of grace and truth" *John 1:14.*

SHARPER IMAGE

Julia Bluhm couldn't believe it. Most of the girls in her ballet class complained about being fat. They weren't. They were healthy, active, growing girls who only felt that way because they compared themselves to the models they saw in magazines and on TV. The eighth grader from Maine told her friends they were beautiful, but she didn't stop there. In 2012 Julia created an online petition to encourage *Seventeen* magazine to publish *one* unaltered picture per month. All magazines tend to Photoshop their images, making perfect-looking models look even more "perfect" by thinning them out and smoothing their skin. At the beginning of summer, Julia showed up in front of *Seventeen* magazine's offices in New York City with more than 84,000 signatures of people who agreed with her.

In the August 2012 issue of *Seventeen*, the magazine announced it would never use Photoshop to change the body and face shapes of its models and always feature photos of real girls who are healthy.

We live in an image-obsessed culture. About 80 percent of fifteen- to twenty-five-year-olds would like to alter something about their bodies. Many feel being beautiful would make them popular. But instead of a change in appearance, most people just need a change of attitude. The Bible tells us that Jesus wasn't attractive, yet thousands of people were drawn to him.

EXAMINE THE CASE

Isaiah 53:2 says the Messiah would have "no beauty or majesty to attract us to him, nothing in his appearance that we should desire him." In other words, Jesus didn't attract followers with his good looks. People came to Jesus because he put others above himself. He demonstrated God's love with his words and actions. And he was confident about God's plan for his life.

Jesus didn't stand out because of his appearance. He was most likely sort of short and common looking. But he was kind, honest, caring, and helpful. As you read about Jesus in the Gospels, highlight places where he shows those characteristics. You'll end up with a colorful Bible.

As you interact with people in your world, it's important to present yourself well by being clean and well groomed. But be careful not to get caught up in popular culture. Jesus didn't. He stood out in other ways to develop lasting friendships and build popularity. You can do the same.

FINAL WORD

"He had no beauty or majesty to attract us to him, nothing in his appearance that we should desire him" *Isaiah 53:2.*

EYEWITNESS ACCOUNT

Ryan saw the whole thing: Connor knocked Kaylee's lunch out of her hands on purpose. Pizza and tater tots littered the cafeteria floor.

Ryan ran to the lunchroom monitor and told her that Kaylee had been laughing with friends when Connor caused a collision. At the same time, Hannah ran to the monitor to complain that Kaylee wasn't paying attention and got in Connor's way. Now Connor's neck hurt.

"That's not what happened," Ryan said. "Connor knocked Kaylee's lunch out of her hands on purpose."

"He did not," Hannah answered. "It was Kaylee's fault."

Whose story is true? The answer could be *both*. Although Hannah and Ryan viewed things differently, each accurately told what they saw.

For years, psychologists and law enforcement professionals have studied the problem with eyewitness testimony. In Great Britain, police set up a fake crime in a restaurant and had ten volunteers watch and recount what happened. The differences in the testimonies were staggering, yet everybody was telling the truth.

EXAMINE THE CASE

Maybe you've heard people say the Bible isn't true because of differences in the same Gospel stories. The Gospels of Jesus' life were written from eyewitness accounts (Luke 1:2). Luke 9 and Mark 9 tell similar stories. In Luke 9:50 Jesus is quoted as saying, "For whoever is not against you is for you." Jesus' quote in Mark 9:39–40 is a sentence longer and from a different point of view. Does that prove the Bible is full of errors? Not at all.

Bible scholar Daniel B. Wallace once had a young woman from another religion approach him with six handwritten pages of supposed discrepancies in the Gospels. "You're going to have to answer every single one of these before I can believe anything about Christianity," she said.

"Don't you think this list proves that the writers didn't conspire and collude when they wrote their Gospels?" Wallace answered.

Wallace went on to point out that the core message of the Gospels—Jesus performed miracles, healed people, forgave sins, prophesied his own death and resurrection, died on a cross, and rose from the dead—is exactly the same in all accounts.

Two weeks later, this young woman gave her life to Christ.

The Gospels all recount the life of Jesus through their own perspectives—and that's testimony you can trust.

FINAL WORD

"Many have undertaken to draw up an account of the things that have been fulfilled among us, just as they were handed down to us by those who from the first were eyewitnesses and servants of the word" *Luke 1:1–2*.

MORE THAN A FRIEND

How many names do you have? Most people have three—a first, middle, and last. In 2012 a woman in Great Britain set a world record by legally changing her name to include 161 names! That's a lot, but Jesus was known by even more. He was called the Son of God, Holy One, King, Emmanuel, Prince of Peace, Messiah, Master, Lamb of God, Bread of Life, Rock, Deliverer, and the names go on and on. All of Jesus' names have a special meaning and allow you to know more about his character. He's the Chief Shepherd and your Advocate.

Similarly, your names give people an idea of who you are. Do you know the meaning of your name? If not, ask a parent to tell you what it means. In addition to your given name, you're probably known by many other names: student, child, brother or sister, athlete, musician, and friend. Jesus even calls you "friend." John 15:15 says, "I have called you friends, for everything that I learned from my Father I have made known to you." It's nice to think about Jesus being your friend, but he's a lot more than that.

EXAMINE THE CASE

Bible scholar Daniel B. Wallace believes Christians need to do two things to grow in depth and understanding of their faith.

"First, we have to quit marginalizing scripture," he says. "We really need to wrestle with the issues, because our faith depends on it. And second, we need to quit turning Jesus into our buddy. He's the sovereign Lord of the universe, and we need to understand that and respond accordingly." Christian writer C. S. Lewis may have explained it best. When he described Aslan, the lion who symbolizes Jesus Christ in the Chronicles of Narnia books, Lewis wrote, "'Course he isn't safe. But he's good. He's the King."

Not surprisingly, one of Jesus' names is Lion of the Tribe of Judah (Revelation 5:5). He is powerful, good ... and a little dangerous. Jesus is the most powerful name in the history of the world. Just the mention of his name causes people to bow in reverence (Philippians 2:10). We should show similar reverence as we serve Christ and interact with him through prayer. He is, after all, the King of Kings.

FINAL WORD

"At the name of Jesus every knee should bow, in heaven and on earth and under the earth, and every tongue acknowledge that Jesus Christ is Lord" *Philippians 2:10–11.*

COMPLETE CLEANUP

You probably don't love to wash the dishes. But dishwashing soap can be fun. Don't believe it? Just try this experiment. Gather a shallow plate or bowl, a little bit of water, some black pepper, and a drop of dishwashing soap.

Start by pouring some water into the bowl. Sprinkle pepper all over the surface of the water. Dip your finger into the water. What happens? Maybe a few waves, right? Now dab some dishwashing liquid onto your finger. Put that finger into the bowl and voilà! The pepper rushes to the edge of the dish. All you can see now is clear water. Amazing, huh?

While this fun experiment can teach you something about the scientific principle of surface tension, it's also a vivid picture of what Christ does to sin in our life.

EXAMINE THE CASE

Before we pray to ask Jesus to be our Savior, our lives are peppered with sin. We can attempt to clean ourselves up by dipping our finger into acting nicer or speaking more kindly, but nothing truly works. Maybe we see a small effect for a short time, but we'll never see any ultimate change without God. Only Christ can clean up our lives. Just like when soap hits the water, when Jesus enters our lives our sins are instantly pushed away. Psalm 103:12 says, "As far as the east is from the west, so far has he removed our transgressions from us."

Think about the statement, "as far as the east is from the west." God doesn't just remove our sins to the edge of the dish; he wipes them clean off the planet. Our sins are removed altogether. They're totally forgiven. Because of Jesus, we can stand before God as redeemed and holy.

If your family hasn't seen the pepper trick, gather them together in the kitchen. Demonstrate how the soap clears the pepper from the surface of the water. Explain the similarities in how Jesus cleans up our lives. Then take a few minutes as a family to pray and thank Jesus for coming to earth so our sins can be forgiven. That was no trick. Just a complete cleanup.

FINAL WORD

"As far as the east is from the west, so far has he removed our transgressions from us" *Psalm 103:12*.

TAKE THE
PLUNGE

How do you get into a swimming pool? Some people dip in their toes to test the water's temperature. Others walk to the shallow end and slowly ease themselves into the water. Then there are those who leap off the side of the pool and do a cannonball into the deep end.

In the early 1980s, cannonballs were more than a way to jump into the water. They were a source of competition at the World Belly-Flop and Cannonball Diving Championships. Contestants dressed in funny costumes and bright bathing suits, hoping to make a big splash. Each competitor— some weighed over 250 pounds—performed three jumps from a one-meter diving board where they earned points based on six criteria: height of splash, water displaced from pool, degree of difficulty, artistry, personality, and color of swimsuit. The winner received an amazing array of prizes, including a green bathroom, a trophy, a bowling bag, a set of wrenches, and a bag of cash. Not to mention bragging rights as the world's best cannonballer.

EXAMINE THE CASE

A silly contest might appear to have little to do with our faith in Christ. But when it comes to following Jesus, he wants us to dive in! Dipping your toe into Christianity can be an okay way to start, but until you take the plunge and give your whole life to Christ, your faith can leave you feeling cold.

During Jesus' time on earth, a teacher of the law asked him which of the commandments was the most important. Jesus answered, "Love the Lord your God with all your heart and with all your soul and with all your mind and with all your strength" (Mark 12:30). Notice that Jesus said *all* your heart, *all* your soul, *all* your mind, and *all* your strength. We can't effectively live for Christ when we just dip in our toes. Doing a cannonball into a life with Jesus Christ can seem scary. You might risk people thinking you're a little weird. But in reality, diving into your relationship with God isn't risky at all. When you take the plunge and wholeheartedly commit to Christ, you're guaranteed to never belly-flop but always make a big splash.

FINAL WORD

"Love the Lord your God with all your heart and with all your soul and with all your mind and with all your strength" *Mark 12:30.*

AT THE CROSS

You've seen the picture before. Three crosses silhouetted on a hill. All appears peaceful and calm.

The scene at the actual cross where Jesus died was anything but calm. It was gruesome, sad, horrible ... and yet awe-inspiring. After being beaten by Roman soldiers, Jesus was forced to carry his cross up the hill to Golgotha. He was too weak to make it, so soldiers grabbed somebody from the crowd to take Jesus' cross to the top. He was nailed to the wooden beams and lifted into the air. Breathing was difficult. Talking strained. Yet Jesus managed to look down at his mother and tell one of his disciples to care for her. Jesus heard the taunts from soldiers and the criminals being executed next to him. When one of those men recognized the truth of who Jesus was, Jesus told him, "Truly I tell you, today you will be with me in paradise." Jesus forgave those who tortured him, cried out to God, and died on that rough cross.

Was it a terrible scene? Yes. Was it also magnificent? Absolutely.

EXAMINE THE CASE

Some books have been written that say Jesus merely fainted on the cross and then revived in the tomb. That's simply not true. Numerous historians report Jesus died. The Romans were good at many things—killing was one of them. The soldiers at the cross made sure Jesus was dead before taking him down. Talking about Jesus' death is sad, but it's also necessary. Jesus came to die for our sins so that we could live. He was the ultimate sacrificial lamb. John 3:16 tells us, "For God so loved the world that he gave his one and only Son, that whoever believes in him shall not perish but have eternal life."

Have you prayed to ask Jesus to be your Savior? He suffered so you could be forgiven. If you've never prayed to give your life to Christ, you can do that right now by saying: "Jesus, I'm sorry for all the times I've sinned by doing what I wanted instead of following your rules. I believe you took my punishment and suffered in my place by dying on the cross. Help me to follow you. Please come into my life. Thank you for saving me. Amen."

If you just prayed that prayer, go tell someone. A parent, a youth pastor, the person who gave you this book. Then commit to learning more about Jesus and serving him with your life.

FINAL WORD

"For God so loved the world that he gave his one and only Son, that whoever believes in him shall not perish but have eternal life" *John 3:16*.

HELD TOGETHER

As science and technology advance, so does our understanding of God's design for our bodies and the world around us. In 1979 scientists Rupert Timpl and George R. Martin discovered a substance they called *laminin*. Think of it as body glue. Basically, laminin holds our cells together. Without laminin every tissue of every living thing wouldn't stay together. It's a microscopic key to our survival.

In a paper published in the *Journal of Biological Chemistry*, Timpl and Martin said laminin "consisted of at least two polypeptide chains joined to each other by disulfide bonds." *Say what?* While the science sounds confusing, when you see what laminin looks like, its power becomes clear. Scientists who study the human cell under incredibly powerful electron microscopes have found that all laminins discovered so far are in a cross-like shape. So the protein that holds our cells together looks like a cross.

Pastor Louie Giglio is a popular author and speaker who talks about amazing creations that reflect God's handiwork. Search for "Louie Giglio" on YouTube for awesome information on laminin and more.

"How crazy is that," said pastor Louie Giglio. "The stuff

that holds our bodies together, that's holding the linings of your organs together, that's holding your skin on, is in the shape of the cross of our Lord Jesus Christ."

EXAMINE THE CASE

God's design, love, and power display themselves in all of creation—even in places that the human eye cannot see. God's fingerprints are on everything. He even holds our bodies together with the symbol of his never-failing love. In Colossians 1:16–17 the apostle Paul wrote, "For in him all things were created: things in heaven and on earth, visible and invisible. He is before all things, and in him all things hold together." Paul probably had no idea about laminin. But he had a rock-solid faith based on the cross of Jesus Christ.

As you go through life, you'll probably experience times of doubt in your Christian faith. You may hear a teacher discredit Christ, see a TV show that argues against Christianity, or experience a time when God feels far away. When that happens, remember to look at the cross. The cross holds our Christian faith together, just like cross-shaped laminin holds our cells together. Jesus gave his life so we can be forgiven and know God personally. Without the cross, we could never have that bond. So hold on to the cross, and hold close to Christ.

FINAL WORD

"For in him all things were created: things in heaven and on earth, visible and invisible. He is before all things, and in him all things hold together" *Colossians 1:16–17*.

FOUNDATION OF FAITH

What's your favorite toy of all time? According to a global survey, LEGO building bricks top the list. LEGOs placed first for boys and were in the top three for girls, easily making them the overall winner. After being founded as a wooden toy manufacturer in 1932, LEGO began making its current design of plastic bricks in 1958. More than 400 billion LEGOs have been created since that time. Nineteen billion are molded each year, which means 36,000 blocks are produced every minute.

In September 2012 a group in the Czech Republic celebrated LEGO's eightieth anniversary by building the world's tallest LEGO tower. The tradition of creating massive LEGO structures began with a fifty-foot tower built in London in 1988. Since then the record has been broken by teams in Canada, Austria, Germany, Brazil, France, the United States, Japan, Denmark, and South Korea—to name just a few. From September 5 to 9, volunteers in Prague constructed a tower that measured nearly 107 feet tall! In all, about 500,000 LEGOs were used in the massive structure.

EXAMINE THE CASE

How was the tallest LEGO tower built? Brick by brick. The same thing is true about your life with Christ. When you accept Jesus as your Savior, it's like laying the cornerstone of your faith. The Bible calls Jesus the cornerstone and says anyone who trusts in the cornerstone will never be put to shame (1 Peter 2:6).

The most important stone in any building is the cornerstone. It's the first stone that's put down and is perfectly level and square. Every stone in the building must line up with the cornerstone. As you put together what you believe, make sure every "stone" lines up with the cornerstone of Christ. Test every idea you hear against Jesus' standards. Look to him as you decide what's right and wrong. Learn to follow his commands. Seek his will in every decision you make.

When the people around you know you're a Christian, they'll watch you to see what it means to follow Jesus. Build a towering life that honors God. Stand tall for Jesus. By starting your life on the firm foundation of Jesus Christ, you won't crack and crumble under the pressures of the world.

FINAL WORD

"For in Scripture it says: 'See, I lay a stone in Zion, a chosen and precious cornerstone, and the one who trusts in him will never be put to shame'" *1 Peter 2:6*.

SWEET TREAT

Sweet things can be good for you. (Just don't tell your dentist.) A study at the University of California, San Diego, discovered that people who regularly eat chocolate weigh less—five to seven pounds on average—than those who stay away from the sweet. An ounce or two a day can be a great treat. Dark chocolate is even better for you. Research shows if you eat chocolate that contains 70 percent cocoa, you enjoy health benefits along with the yumminess. Small amounts of dark chocolate can put you in a better mood, boost your body's ability to fight disease, and help harden your teeth. Plus, it contains helpful minerals, like potassium, copper, magnesium, and iron.

But dark chocolate isn't the only treat that's sweet for your body. For thousands of years, people have known about the health benefits of honey. Research shows honey has antibacterial and antifungal properties, reduces the risk of some cancers, helps with coughs, aids in healing wounds, and gives you better skin.

EXAMINE THE CASE

Numerous times in the Bible, God's Word is compared to honey. And the sweetness of God's Word always comes out on top. We normally relate sweet things with dessert or a reward. And that's exactly how we should view God's Word. We should desire to taste the sweetness of God as much as possible. His Word is sweet and good for us. Proverbs 24:14 reminds us, "Wisdom is like honey for you: If you find it, there is a future hope for you." And the best place to find wisdom is in the Bible.

If we're honest, we may have to admit that we don't look at reading the Bible in the same way as biting into a Reese's Dark Chocolate Peanut Butter Cup. But we should. Think of some ways you can make studying God's Word sweet. Maybe you could keep a journal of what you learn. Or you could draw pictures of the stories you're reading about. You could even make up a song or poem. Get excited about getting into God's Word in the same way you would crave a bite of chocolate. Just remember to brush your teeth afterward ... eating sweets, that is, not reading the Bible.

FINAL WORD

"How sweet are your words to my taste, sweeter than honey to my mouth" *Psalm 119:103*.

REALITY CHECK

Avery didn't like to be cold. She celebrated for a week when her parents said they were moving to Hawaii. Now she could be warm all the time. She liked warmth so much that she never put anything in the refrigerator. *What's the big deal with coldness?* Avery thought. *Being warm is much better.* Her parents tried to tell her about bacteria and how food would spoil, but she didn't believe it. She couldn't see bacteria, so how could it exist?

> Our beliefs don't change reality.

But one day Avery grabbed the milk from the counter and poured it on her cereal. To her surprise, it came out in huge, stinky globs. Then she decided to make a turkey sandwich. It didn't smell much better, and the cheese was covered in green mold.

What happened? Avery discovered an important lesson: Our beliefs don't change reality.

EXAMINE THE CASE

Avery sincerely believed refrigeration was a bad thing, and she was sincerely wrong. Many people have misguided and unfounded beliefs about Jesus. Paul Copan has studied the claims of Christ for years and written or edited over a dozen books, including *True for You But Not for Me*. "I can't stress this enough," Copan said. "What we believe about Jesus doesn't affect who he is. Whether we choose to believe it or not, Jesus is the unique Son of God ... So we have a choice: we can live in a fantasyland of our own making by believing whatever we want about him; or we can seek to discover who he really is."

You can't see Jesus, but you can trust that "Jesus Christ is the same yesterday and today and forever" (Hebrews 13:8). Although he doesn't change, our understanding of him should grow and deepen. But how do we discover more about Jesus?

One of the best ways to find out who Jesus is, what he did, and his true character is by reading the Gospels—Matthew, Mark, Luke, and John. Choose one of the Gospels to read each day as you go through this devotional book. (Hint: Mark is the shortest, but all of the Gospels contain great facts about Christ.) Write down which book you want to read here:

• • •

Try to read one chapter a day. When you seek after the reality of Jesus, your understanding of what's *really* real will become clearer as well.

FINAL WORD

"Jesus Christ is the same yesterday and today and forever" *Hebrews 13:8*).

HEART OF
THE MATTER

Look at your hand and make a fist. That's about the size of your heart. Protected by your ribs, this muscle weighs as much as an apple. Yet this amazing organ beats around 100,000 times a day and pumps more than 2,000 gallons of blood every twenty-four hours. Nearly 60,000 miles of blood vessels weave throughout your body, delivering blood packed with life-giving oxygen and nutrients to all of your organs and tissues.

Some blood vessels, such as the aorta, can be pretty big. The aorta connects to the heart and is the largest artery in the body, measuring as big around as a garden hose. But it takes ten capillaries, the smallest blood vessel, to equal the width of a human hair!

EXAMINE THE CASE

God's design of the circulatory system is amazingly complex and powerful. But without a heart, it doesn't work. If you remove your heart, your body dies. In the same way, if you remove Jesus Christ from Christianity, then the faith is dead. Craig A. Evans, PhD, founded the Dead Sea Scrolls Institute and has written or edited more than fifty books about Christianity. Evans says the heart of Christianity can be summed up in two words: Jesus Christ.

"So the core message of Christianity . . . is that Jesus is the Messiah," Evans said. "He's God's Son, he fulfills the scriptures, he died on the cross . . . saved humanity, he rose from the dead."

Christ is the key to the Christian life—just like the heart is key for physical life. And when you put Jesus and your heart together, you get eternal life. In Ephesians 3:17 the apostle Paul writes, "Then Christ will make his home in your hearts as you trust in him. Your roots will grow down into God's love and keep you strong" (NLT).

Isn't it amazing to think that Jesus lives in you? The author of life gives you life and makes you strong. Put your hand over your heart and feel it beating. Then take a moment to pray and thank Jesus for giving you life now and throughout eternity.

FINAL WORD

"Then Christ will make his home in your hearts as you trust in him. Your roots will grow down into God's love and keep you strong" *Ephesians 3:17 NLT.*

NOT THE EASTER BUNNY

Have you ever thought about how strange the tooth fairy is? She sneaks into your room, digs around under your pillow, and steals a bloody tooth. Sure, you receive something in return, but it's still a little creepy. Italy, Spain, and France have a nicer tradition—supposedly a little mouse scurries into your room and takes your teeth. How cute! (Unless you don't like mice next to your face.)

The world is filled with different traditions. In Australia, children pass up chocolate Easter bunnies to buy Easter bilbies—a much-loved, endangered, mini-kangaroo-looking creature. Every Easter sales from chocolate bilbies go toward helping this animal survive.

Christmas can also get a little crazy with its traditions. Forget about Santa Claus. In Denmark, *Sinterklaas* arrives by boat in early December. Instead of putting out cookies for him, children fill a wooden shoe with hay and carrots. The good kids

© Susan Flashman/Shutterstock

get presents. In China, *Dun Che Lao Ren* (which loosely translated means "Christmas Old Man") brings gifts. Try putting that into a song: "Christmas Old Man is coming to town." It just doesn't work. Then there's *Jultomten*. This Swedish gnome brings presents on a sleigh pulled by goats.

EXAMINE THE CASE

Many traditions began with a small piece of history. Then things get exaggerated and mixed up. Some people say that's the case with Jesus. They think, *He's just a myth. No person could do everything that Jesus did.* But when you honestly look at the historical evidence, dig into his claims of being God, and explore the effect he's had on the world and in individual lives, then you'll come to one conclusion: Jesus is no Easter bunny. He's 100 percent real.

Jesus is not just a feel-good symbol who's as irrelevant to your life as the tooth fairy. He's the Son of the living God who saved you from your sins. First Peter 2:24 says, "He personally carried our sins in his body on the cross so that we can be dead to sin and live for what is right. By his wounds you are healed" (NLT). Because of Christ's sacrifice, you can live for what is right. The Easter bunny may bring us chocolate, but Jesus brings us life!

Write down one thing you want to live for:

FINAL WORD

"He personally carried our sins in his body on the cross so that we can be dead to sin and live for what is right. By his wounds you are healed" *1 Peter 2:24 NLT.*

NO BONES ABOUT IT

Bones can talk. Not with words, but they tell a story. Archaeologists can dig up an ancient bone and figure out when that person lived, if they had any vitamin deficiencies, what kind of culture they lived in, and many other facts. So in the late 2000s, Academy Award–winning director James Cameron thought he had an earth-shaking story when he made a documentary that claimed archaeologists had found the box that had contained Jesus' bones. If Jesus died and *didn't* rise from the dead, it would disprove Christianity.

Just one problem—actually one *very big* problem—the bone box didn't belong to Jesus Christ. In 1980, the Talpiot tomb was found in the old city of Jerusalem. Etched on one of the ossuaries, or bone boxes, were some very familiar names: Jesus, son of Joseph, Joseh (Joseph), Maria (Mary), Matia (Matthew), Mariamne Mara (claimed to be Mary Magdalene), and Judah, son of Jesus. The movie claimed Jesus had married Mary Magdalene and they had at least one child together. Then they all died and were buried as a family. The movie played on a major cable TV station. Millions watched and received a mixed-up message.

EXAMINE THE CASE

Maybe it made some people question the Bible's account of Jesus, but experts were unimpressed. Amos Kloner, the archaeologist who oversaw the Talpiot tomb's excavation, said, "It makes for a great TV film, but it's completely impossible. It's nonsense."

While the names sound credible, they were far too common to prove anything conclusive. Mary was the most popular name during Jesus' time. One out of every five women in Jerusalem was named Mary. Similarly, one out of every seven men in Jerusalem was named Joseph. Jesus, Judah, and Matthew were also extremely common names. Plus, Mary Magdalene was never referred to as "Mariamne Mara." All of that evidence, plus numerous other details, caused experts, including Kloner, to say, "The possibility of it being Jesus' family [is] very close to zero." There could have been a Jesus buried there, but it's *not* Jesus Christ, God's Son.

Whenever "new" discoveries appear that claim to disprove the Bible, make sure to explore the facts before jumping to conclusions. In this case, you can trust the angel at Jesus' tomb who told the women, "I know that you are looking for Jesus, who was crucified. He is not here; he has risen, just as he said."

FINAL WORD

"I know that you are looking for Jesus, who was crucified. He is not here; he has risen, just as he said" *Matthew 28:5–6.*

START
SPREADING
THE NEWS

How do you find out what's going on in the world? It's probably a lot different than how your parents or grandparents got the news. Since the beginning of 2011, research shows more people read the news on their smartphones and computers than in newspapers. But can you trust everything you read on the Internet? A character on a popular TV comedy once said, "Wikipedia is the best thing ever. Anyone in the world can write anything they want about any subject. So you know you are getting the best possible information."

Does that sound like a true statement? As helpful as the Internet can be, obviously you can't trust everything you read on it. A lot of false information can get posted and reposted on a variety of sites. That's why most teachers don't allow Wikipedia to be used as a source for research papers. You have to check your sources and make sure the facts are reliable.

EXAMINE THE CASE

God's Word is reliable. For thousands of years, it has passed the truth test. And it contains the best kind of news—God's good news. Jesus Christ came to the world to fulfill God's promise to send a Savior to save us from our sins. How cool is that? If Jesus walked the earth today, he'd grab headlines in newspapers and on the Internet. MAN HEALS PERSON BORN LAME. MIRACLE WORKER AT IT AGAIN: FEEDS 5,000. GRAVE EMPTY: JESUS SEEN WALKING COUNTRYSIDE. Jesus himself said his coming was big news: "'The time has come,' he said. 'The kingdom of God has come near. Repent and believe the good news!'" (Mark 1:15). Once you understand the truth of that statement, your life is never the same. That's more good news about the Good News. Jesus doesn't want you to keep this news to yourself; he wants you to share it with others.

Think again about how you get your news. One of your first thoughts was probably, *From my friends.* We naturally trust what our friends tell us because of our relationship with them. Do you have any friends who don't have a personal relationship with Jesus? Have you told them the good news? Write down the name of one friend you want to tell about God's good news:

• • •

Now commit to actually do it.

FINAL WORD

"'The time has come,' he said. 'The kingdom of God has come near. Repent and believe the good news!'" *Mark 1:15.*

BE SHARP

Snow-covered mountains whizzed by. Carter couldn't wait to get out of the car. This year his dad was going to let him chop down a Christmas tree. Not his family's Christmas tree. Dad would chop down that one. But a neighbor had offered to pay Carter to bring him back a tree.

Dad guided the car off the highway and onto a dirt road. He pulled to a stop, got out, and grabbed two axes. Almost immediately, Carter found the perfect tree. Dad spotted another nice one close by. He handed his son an axe.

"Let's see who can cut down his tree the fastest," Carter said.

Carter ran to his tree and started to chop with fury. First, he removed some of the lower branches to get to the trunk. Then he hacked with gusto. Every so often, Carter glanced at his dad, who was working at a steady pace. Carter even saw him take a break while cradling his axe.

I took time to sharpen my blade.

He's probably praying that he'll beat me, Carter thought with a smile.

Moments later, Carter heard his dad's tree crack and fall to the ground. Carter was less than halfway done.

"How did you beat me?" Carter yelled. "I didn't even take a break."

"You worked really hard," Dad said, "but I took time to sharpen my blade."

EXAMINE THE CASE

Exerting a lot of effort doesn't always lead to an effective life for Christ. You need to make sure your blade is sharp. Ecclesiastes 10:10 says, "If the ax is dull, and one does not sharpen its edge, then one must exert more strength; however, the advantage of wisdom is that it brings success" (HCSB). So how can you be wise when it comes to living for Jesus?

One of the best ways is to find a friend who shares your beliefs. Do you know somebody who loves God and wants to grow in their relationship with Jesus? Maybe you could ask to be accountability partners. Meet regularly to find out what God is teaching you, pray for each other, and talk about problems and successes. If you can't think of a good accountability partner, ask your mom, dad, or youth pastor. Proverbs 27:17 tells us it's important to have somebody in our lives to make us sharper.

Our own individual efforts can only get us so far. Instead of working harder, we need to work smarter and find a friend who can help us grow closer to Christ.

FINAL WORD

"As iron sharpens iron, so one person sharpens another" *Proverbs 27:17.*

REWARDS OF PATIENCE

How long would you wait in order to get two marshmallows instead of one? Researchers at the University of Rochester (N.Y.) tested a group of kids ages three to five to see how long they could resist eating this gooey treat. The children were placed in a room in front of a marshmallow. They were promised another marshmallow if they could wait to eat the first one. Then the researcher left the room for fifteen minutes. The kids had no idea when the researcher would return. Some kids licked the marshmallow. Others tried looking away. Some picked tiny pieces from it, and a few just popped the whole thing in their mouth without waiting.

For a little fun, search for "Marshmallow Temptation extended version" on the Internet and watch the five-minute video on YouTube.

To make the experiment more interesting, before entering the room the children were divided into two groups. Both groups started doing a craft project with broken crayons and poor art supplies. The researchers promised each group they'd return with better supplies. For one group of kids, they came back with brand-new crayons and cool stickers. Researchers returned to the other group empty-handed. The kids who received the better art supplies, as promised, waited an average of twelve minutes before eating the marshmallow. The group who experienced disappointment in not receiving better supplies only waited an average of three minutes.

EXAMINE THE CASE

Waiting can be hard, even if you know you'll receive a reward. As Christians, we're encouraged to wait for the Lord's timing. But nobody likes to wait. It's hard enough to wait three minutes for microwave popcorn—let alone days, weeks, or months for God to answer a prayer. We want instant gratification. We want to eat the marshmallow now!

King David didn't always wait on the Lord, but his life went much better when he did. In Psalm 27:13–14 he says, "I remain confident of this: I will see the goodness of the Lord in the land of the living. Wait for the Lord; be strong and take heart and wait for the Lord." Sometimes you might be tempted to take a shortcut or get something done on your own power. But God always comes through on his promises. If you wait, you'll end up with something *much better* than two marshmallows. His plans are greater than your plans, so always wait on the Lord and experience his blessings.

FINAL WORD

"I wait for the Lord, my whole being waits, and in his word I put my hope" *Psalm 130:5.*

TREACHEROUS TOYS AND YOU

Toys are meant to be fun, but sometimes they can be downright dangerous. What were toy creators thinking when they put these products on shelves?

- Disney Princess Racing Trike. This pink plastic three-wheeler sold from 2009 to 2011. Was it pretty? Yes, its purple wheels and fuchsia handlebars were a hit. Was it dangerous? Definitely. It probably should've come with a pair of safety goggles. For some reason, makers put a pointy castle and three small-headed princesses on the steering wheel. One quick stop or an accidental trip, and kids would end up with a face full of pain. Around 10,000 trikes sold in the United States and Canada before the toymakers got smart and sent out replacement handlebars that didn't feature the pokey castle and princesses.
- Lucky Star Submarine Stationery Set. This little submarine sold in the late 1980s and was perfect for helping kids do their schoolwork. Just one problem: In addition to the tape dispenser, pencil sharpener, and drawers for pencils and markers, it also contained a hidden razor blade cutting tool. Putting razor blades in the hands of little children is definitely not a good

idea. Fortunately, these subs only sold for a three-month period before being recalled.

EXAMINE THE CASE

Aren't you glad God created you, instead of some toymaker? All of God's creations are perfect. Not that we're perfect, but through the help of the Holy Spirit, we should be working toward perfection.

In Philippians 3:12 Paul tells us, "I don't mean to say ... that I have already reached perfection. But I press on to possess that perfection for which Christ Jesus first possessed me" (NLT). Like the old saying goes, "Jesus doesn't make any junk." But we all have areas where we can improve. Maybe you have a bad temper, or you procrastinate, or you have a tendency to be selfish. As you grow closer to Jesus, you become more like him. And he is perfect.

You'll never be recalled or need replacement parts, but that doesn't mean you should stay in your current condition. When Christ came into your life, you became "new and improved." As God continues his work in you, your goal should be to keep improving.

FINAL WORD

"I don't mean to say that I have already achieved these things or that I have already reached perfection. But I press on to possess that perfection for which Christ Jesus first possessed me" *Philippians 3:12 NLT.*

ARE YOU SMARTER THAN ...?

Ken Jennings is smart. The computer software engineer from Salt Lake City, Utah, has won more money on game shows than anybody in the history of TV. He started his winning on the quiz show *Jeopardy!* From June 2 through November 30, 2004, Ken won seventy-five straight games and earned $2,522,700! But Ken wasn't done yet. He won an additional $500,000 in a *Jeopardy* tournament of champions. Then he appeared on *Are You Smarter Than a 5th Grader?* and took home another $500,000. He became so popular that other game shows invited him to appear. Eventually his total winnings grew to $3,773,414.29.

Part of that money came from the *Jeopardy! IBM Challenge* in February 2011 where Ken and Brad Rutter (who has won nearly $3.5 million on game shows) played against "Watson," a computer programmed to understand common language. Watson had an advantage in that it held four terabytes of information—that's the same as 4,000 gigabytes or about as much as twenty normal computers. All the text from Wikipedia was stored on its hard drive. In the end, Ken and Brad were no match for Watson. The computer won the two-round tournament with more than $77,000. Ken placed second with

$24,000 (he could've had much more, but played it safe on the Final Jeopardy question), while Brad came in third.

EXAMINE THE CASE

Ken Jennings has an amazing mind. Watson's knowledge is even more impressive. But neither comes close to the mind of God. Simply put, he knows everything (1 John 3:20). He's known everything from the beginning of time, and he even knows the future.

As you discover more about God, you'll learn that he's omniscient, omnipotent, and omnipresent. Those are just big words that mean God is all-knowing, all-powerful, and present everywhere at the same time. God's Word tells us that his knowledge is limitless. Nothing can be hidden from him. He searches our hearts and knows our thoughts. Jesus knew Judas would betray him. Jesus also knew that he'd rise from the dead. God has all the answers to our questions and all the wisdom of the universe.

If you knew about a website with all the answers to life's questions on it, what would you do? You'd probably search it out. Well, God *is* that website. And you don't even need to Google him. His knowledge is absolute. As you grow, you'll probably become smarter than a fifth grader, but you'll never be smarter than God.

FINAL WORD

"We know that God is greater than our hearts, and he knows everything" *1 John 3:20.*

LIVING LARGE

What's the largest living thing on earth? Your first guess might be the blue whale. It's the largest *animal* ever known. These massive mammals grow up to 100 feet long and can weigh 200 tons. (That's 400,000 pounds!) Blue whales are so big their tongues weigh as much as an elephant, and their hearts can weigh more than a car.

But blue elephants are far from the largest things on earth. Scientists found a mushroom colony in Oregon that spans about six square miles. That's one humongous fungus! While some of the fungus grows underground, plenty of mushrooms can be found poking through the soil. Experts estimate this honey fungus weighs as much as 605 tons. But that's not the largest living organism either. Aspen trees spread through an intricate root system. One tree shoots out its roots and other trees pop up that are identical to the first. Lots of them. Several years ago a scientist found an aspen grove in Utah, where one tree spread over 106 acres. Its estimated weight: 6,000 tons (that's 13 million pounds— way more than a blue whale). The scientist named the aspen "Pando," which is a Latin word meaning "to spread."

EXAMINE THE CASE

Pando is big ... but nowhere close to God's bigness. He doesn't just span across part of a state; he spreads across the universe! God is omnipresent. He's everywhere, all of the time. In Psalm 139 King David writes, "Where can I flee from your presence? If I go up to the heavens, you are there; if I make my bed in the depths, you are there." David goes on to say that no matter where he goes, God is there to guide him.

When Jesus came to earth, he took on human form. But God is not like us. He's a spirit. It's not like God can be found in a rock or the trees (although some movies may urge you to believe that). God is living large, because he's alive everywhere. So look for him, discover his bigness, and be amazed.

FINAL WORD

"Where can I flee from your presence? If I go up to the heavens, you are there; if I make my bed in the depths, you are there. If I rise on the wings of the dawn, if I settle on the far side of the sea, even there your hand will guide me, your right hand will hold me fast" *Psalm 139:7–10*.

ROCK ON

Some people may try to trip up your faith by asking tricky questions. When they hear that God is omnipotent, or all-powerful, they ask, "Well, could God create a rock so big that he couldn't lift it? If God can do anything, certainly he could do that, right?"

Although God is all-powerful, there are several things he *can't* do. For instance, he can't cease to exist. God has been around from the beginning of time and will live forever. God also can't change his nature. The Bible tells us Jesus is the same yesterday, today, and forever (Hebrews 13:8). You can trust that God will never change his rules. He's consistent and solid. He'll always love you and always be there for you.

But what about the rock? As an all-powerful being, God could create an impossibly big rock. Then, because he can do anything requiring power, he'd lift the stone. The rock couldn't be infinite, because only God is infinite—so it's logically impossible for God to create a rock he couldn't lift.

EXAMINE THE CASE

Huh? Sometimes questions can be confusing. Here's something that's not. If anybody asks you the rock question, respond with one of your own: "What kind of God would you want to follow—

one that's in the rock-lifting business or one that's in the stone-rolling business?" God rolled away the stone in front of Jesus Christ's grave when he rose from the dead. Jesus defeated death, which shows a lot more power than lifting rocks.

At times you may be asked some tough questions about your faith, such as *Why does a good God allow bad things to happen?* There are no easy answers to life's difficult questions. As humans, we won't always understand why something happens. But we can always trust that God has a purpose. And all of his purposes are good.

More than fifty times in the Bible, God is called almighty. That means he's *all* mighty. Nothing is more powerful than him. In Job 42:2 Job says to God, "I know that you can do all things; no purpose of yours can be thwarted." Do bad things happen in the world? Are there terrible accidents and natural disasters? Yes. But God's purposes can be accomplished in the good times and bad. Job experienced that firsthand. He suffered unthinkable losses, yet he never doubted God's power. We can follow Job's example by always trusting in God's power and goodness. There's no limit on God's power, and that rocks!

FINAL WORD

"I know that you can do all things; no purpose of yours can be thwarted" *Job 42:2.*

ALIVE AND AWESOME

Jocelyn awoke to the sound of crashing and breaking. "Hey! Can you keep it down?" the ten-year-old yelled groggily. "I'm trying to sleep in here!"

She'd just returned to Chile with her mother and sister. Her dad and older brothers were still in the United States. She couldn't understand why her sister was being so loud this early in the morning. What Jocelyn didn't realize was that an earthquake was creating all the noise.

Suddenly her mom burst into her room. "Come stand in the doorway with me," she said. Her mom said Jesus would take care of them. Once the earth stopped moving, they weren't hurt, but the electricity and phones didn't work. When Jocelyn wrote to Focus on the Family's *Clubhouse* magazine about the 2010 event, she said her mom was worried because she wanted everybody to know they were safe. They prayed God would make a way for them to communicate with their loved ones. Just then a man from their church knocked on the door. He let Jocelyn's mom go to his house to call her dad, brothers, grandma, and aunts. Right after she hung up, the electricity went off in his house.

Some people believe God created everything and then sat back to watch what would happen. That's not what the Bible says.

EXAMINE THE CASE

God is alive and active all over the world. As Paul and Barnabas traveled around spreading God's good news, they told people to turn to the *living* God. God made the heavens and earth, and he continues to show his power by providing for our needs and filling our hearts with joy (Acts 14:17). The living God also shows his love for us by protecting us in dangerous situations and caring about the small details—like he did for Jocelyn's family.

Think about some difficult situations in your life. How did God show up? Maybe he provided for your family financially. Perhaps friends or neighbors rallied around you to help. Or maybe God healed a loved one or performed a miracle. If you take time to look, you will see God actively involved in your life. We don't serve an impersonal, disinterested God. Our God is not only alive and well—he's alive and awesome!

FINAL WORD

"We are bringing you good news, telling you to turn from these worthless things to the living God, who made the heavens and the earth and the sea and everything in them ... He has not left himself without testimony: He has shown kindness by giving you rain from heaven and crops in their seasons; he provides you with plenty of food and fills your hearts with joy"
Acts 14:15, 17.

THAT'S WHY WE PRAY

Don't you love drive-thru restaurants? You pull up to a speaker and shout what you want to eat. Then by the time your parents drive forward in their car, your food is ready to go.

The popular California-based restaurant In-N-Out Burger claims to have created the first drive-thru in 1948 with two-way speakers. Other historians say Red's Giant Hamburg in Springfield, Missouri, had the first drive-thru window. While Red's is long gone, In-N-Out Burger has only increased in popularity with nearly 300 restaurants in five states. Some fans of the fast-food chain love the Bible verses on the food packaging as much as the burgers. Soda cups feature John 3:16 printed on the bottom. Shakes have Proverbs 3:5–6. Hamburger and cheeseburger wrappers point to Revelation 3:20. Hungry people find Nahum 1:7 on double-doubles (that's double the meat and cheese), while Proverbs 24:16 is printed on french fry holders.

Only the references can be found on the In-N-Out products, so if you want to know what the verses say, grab your Bible and look them up.

EXAMINE THE CASE

Some Christians treat God like a drive-thru restaurant. We bow our heads in prayer and give our order. Then we expect God to answer as soon as we "pull forward." And if God doesn't do what we ask, we get angry or think he doesn't hear us.

God always hears our prayers, and he wants us to pray to him about everything. Philippians 4:6 says, "Do not be anxious about anything, but in every situation, by prayer and petition, with thanksgiving, present your requests to God." That means God wants to hear when we're worried about a math test, need wisdom for how to deal with a friend, or desire strength to do well on the athletic field. But prayer is much more than asking for something. When you talk with God, remember this acrostic:

P=Praise. Tell God about the things you're thankful for. Acknowledge his amazing power. Praise him for being active and alive in your life.

R=Repent. Admit your failures. Have you lied, had jealous thoughts, or been selfish? Ask for forgiveness.

A=Ask. Tell God your desires. Ask for his help.

Y=Yield. Let God know that you want to serve him. Tell him that you want to follow his will for your life.

Prayer isn't putting in an order. It's connecting with God, which is much more satisfying.

FINAL WORD

"Do not be anxious about anything, but in every situation, by prayer and petition, with thanksgiving, present your requests to God" *Philippians 4:6*.

CAT TALE THAT NEVER STOPPED

Tracie Steger loves her pets—all seven cats and two dogs. The Spring Hill, Florida, resident took daily walks with her pets to the amazement of her neighbors. None of the pets were on leashes. Steger worked hard to train all of her pets to come when she called, even the cats. Her pets were so well behaved that she often left them outside in her yard to roam around unsupervised. But when Steger called her pets inside for dinner on November 15, 2009, Giggle-Blizzard didn't come. The one-year-old gray kitty was known for his playful attitude but had always been obedient. Steger immediately grabbed her golden retriever and searched for him for hours. The next day she put up "Lost Kitty" signs and posted an announcement on Craigslist.

For more than a week, she didn't hear a thing. Then on Thanksgiving—eleven days later—she heard yowling on her porch. She opened the door, and there was Giggle-Blizzard! His back legs were smashed (probably hit by a car), but he was alive and home. Steger couldn't have been happier. Even two surgeries and $3,000 in veterinarian bills didn't bother her. She was glad to have her kitty back. Giggle-Blizzard showed amazing perseverance. Despite being hit by a car, he dragged himself home on his front legs.

EXAMINE THE CASE

The apostle Paul wrote a lot about suffering. In Romans 5:3–4 he says, "We also glory in our sufferings, because we know that suffering produces perseverance; perseverance, character; and character, hope." Honestly, we usually don't rejoice about suffering; we complain about it. Nobody likes to suffer, yet Jesus promised that we would have trouble in this world as we follow him (John 16:33). But in the midst of our troubles, we can find peace in God's power.

Take a closer look at today's verse. Notice the result of suffering. When we go through a hard time, it teaches us to never give up. That attitude builds our character, because we know that no matter what happens in our lives, we can overcome it with the Lord's help. And all of that leads to hope. Can you remember a time in your life when you learned something through suffering? Talk to a parent or grandparent and ask them the same question. You're sure to hear some amazing stories. God works in our lives in many ways: one of those is through suffering.

FINAL WORD

"We also glory in our sufferings, because we know that suffering produces perseverance; perseverance, character; and character, hope" *Romans 5:3–4.*

GET OUT OF YOUR HEAD

Do you like to run? Most kids do, at least for a short distance. Running around a soccer field is fun. Racing around a track can be a good challenge. But can you imagine running 3,100 miles? And you thought a marathon was long!

Every June since 1997, a group of runners has lined up on a street in Queens, New York, to compete in the longest certified road race in the world. Competitors must finish 3,100 miles in fifty-two days or less. That means they have to run nearly sixty miles a day. Instead of running from New York to Los Angeles (which is about the same distance), runners take 5,649 laps around a city block. Competitors wear through around twenty pairs of shoes as they jog for nearly eighteen hours a day. Breaks include lots of sleeping and lots of eating—around 10,000 calories a day (that's like consuming twenty-three Chick-fil-A sandwiches).

Three thousand miles sounds like a long way, but experts who study human behavior say the longest distance in the world is fourteen inches—the distance between your head and your heart.

EXAMINE THE CASE

Knowing something in your head and having that belief change your life are two very different things. Michael Licona, who wrote *The Case for the Resurrection of Jesus*, says he knows people who acknowledge that Jesus rose from the dead but still refuse to accept Jesus into their hearts. They want to remain the master of their lives instead of giving the throne to God. "In many cases—not all—it's a heart issue, not a head issue," Licona said. "Some people just don't like what Jesus is demanding of them."

Jesus demands our devotion. When we accept Christ as Savior, he becomes Lord of our lives and we are saved from our sins (Romans 10:9). As followers of Christ, we have to do just that ... follow. We must put off selfish desires and live according to God's laws. Your heart is a place of passion. It's what drives you. God wants you to live passionately for him. When your relationship with Christ moves the distance from your head to your heart, your passion for God will shine through.

FINAL WORD

"If you declare with your mouth, 'Jesus is Lord,' and believe in your heart that God raised him from the dead, you will be saved" *Romans 10:9.*

INDISPUTABLE EVIDENCE

If you believe what you watch in movies, a spy's job is to blow up things, escape certain-death situations, capture the bad guy, and use lots of cool gadgets. That just shows you can't trust Hollywood. Most spies spend their time secretly gathering information and sending discoveries to their home country. Their job is to go unnoticed. They need to gather airtight evidence so their country's leaders can make informed decisions. Huge explosions and high-speed chases aren't regular occurrences, but spies do use cool gadgets to gather information.

The International Spy Museum in Washington, DC, features some of the coolest spy gear that's ever been created. For more than forty years, spies have used cameras that look like coat buttons to snap pictures. They've hidden transmitters in the heels of shoes and left messages in fake dog doo (gross, but true). Complicated codes have been used to create, send, and translate information. A camera was even invented that took photos where every shot looked like a tiny dot. But once the dot was magnified, you could see an entire page of information.

Spies do it. Detectives do it. Newspaper reporters do it. People seeking the truth do it. What is it? It's following the facts.

EXAMINE THE CASE

Sometimes in criminal cases all the facts look stacked a certain way. But upon closer investigation, the evidence actually points to the exact opposite conclusion. The case that many people make against the Bible is that way. Those who want to argue against God and his Word will put together evidence that appears convincing at first. But once you dig into the case, you'll find the Bible stands strong.

In 2 Corinthians 10:5 Paul tells us to "demolish arguments and every pretension that sets itself up against the knowledge of God, and we take captive every thought to make it obedient to Christ." If you haven't already, you're bound to meet people and encounter ideas that oppose your belief in God. When that happens, simply follow the facts and you'll find that God's persuasive evidence demolishes all other arguments. Blowing up wrong ideas can be just as fun as blowing up a building ... and it's a lot safer, too.

FINAL WORD

"We demolish arguments and every pretension that sets itself up against the knowledge of God, and we take captive every thought to make it obedient to Christ" *2 Corinthians 10:5*.

SIMPLEMINDED OR FAITH-FILLED

Simple Simon met a skeptic,
Going to the fair.
Said the skeptic to Simple Simon,
"Your God's not anywhere."
Said Simple Simon to the skeptic,
"That's not really true.
Though he's hard to comprehend,
He's as real as me or you."

People who don't believe in Jesus often call Christians simpleminded. They say believing in human reason and the physical sciences makes them more intellectual. Just like the skeptic in the rhyme, they believe God doesn't exist because they can't see him.

It's not simpleminded to believe in Jesus. We put our faith in him because that's the direction that the evidence points. Still, much about God is too big for our minds to understand. How do you explain a God that is one "what" and three "who's." Some have said God's triune nature is like water. Water has three forms—liquid, steam, and ice—yet it's all water. But that's not really an accurate picture because all three persons of the Trinity exist at once—they don't morph from one to the other. Maybe that's why the Bible never uses an illustration to try to explain the Trinity. It simply teaches the Father is God, the Son is God, and the Holy Spirit is God—and that there is one God. That may be the best way to understand it!

EXAMINE THE CASE

If you ever hear somebody say Christians are simpleminded, be ready to stand up for your faith. Some of the greatest scientists and sharpest minds in history believed in God. Plus, followers of Christ shaped the world into what it is today.

Jesus taught his disciples to love everybody. In John 13:34–35 the Lord says, "Just as I have loved you, you should love each other. Your love for one another will prove to the world that you are my disciples" (NLT). Christians have shown love by fighting to end slavery and to get equal rights for women. (Google William Wilberforce or modern-day slavery fighter Zach Hunter.) Followers of Christ have founded the world's largest organizations that help people, such as the Salvation Army, Red Cross, Samaritan's Purse, and World Vision. Believers in Jesus championed education. Of the first 125 universities set up in the United States, nearly all of them had Christian foundations. Early scientists saw God's order in the stars, plant life, and human cells.

By faith, Christians have accomplished amazing things and shown great love ... and that's far from simple.

FINAL WORD

"Just as I have loved you, you should love each other. Your love for one another will prove to the world that you are my disciples" *John 13:34–35 NLT.*

WHAT KIND OF GOGGLES ARE YOU WEARING?

With their big eyes and huge pupils, owls have amazing night vision. Scientists believe owls can spot a mouse running across a field under just a bit of candlelight. (But that begs the question: What's a candle doing in a field?)

If we wanted to see as well as an owl in the dark, we'd need a pair of night-vision goggles. Night-vision goggles were invented during World War II and helped soldiers spot danger in the dark. The technology has changed over the years, but basically the goggles gather and amplify any available light. Some newer goggles can even work in total blackness, because of an infrared illuminator. As you look through the goggles, the images appear green, because the inventors knew the human eye is extra sensitive to that color.

The military frequently uses night-vision technology. Many police forces also rely on the goggles to track down criminals in the dark. But anyone can buy a pair of night-vision goggles for less than $200 to well over $2,000—depending on how high tech you want to get.

EXAMINE THE CASE

Everybody wears goggles. They might not be night-vision goggles, but we all see the world through a particular "lens." When you pray to ask Christ into your life, you become a new creation (2 Corinthians 5:17). At that moment, it's like you put on "God-vision goggles." You stop seeing things the way you used to and start seeing them through God's lens. Instead of looking at purple mountains' majesty, you now see God's majesty in magnificent mountains. Instead of a tiny white blood cell, you see God's design for protecting your body against disease.

As a Christian, you naturally view life through a Christian worldview. Scientists and scholars who don't believe in God see things differently. When people choose to assume there is no God, they miss seeing God's handiwork in the world around them.

When you read articles and books written by various experts, remember to think about the kind of goggles these writers wear. As you read and learn more about the Bible, you can test and approve what is right or wrong according to God's Word. Some scholars only want to disprove the Bible—no matter what the facts say. They can't see God's light, because their goggles block it out. Embrace the best information. Make sure your goggles are tuned into seeing the light in the darkness.

FINAL WORD

"If anyone is in Christ, the new creation has come: The old has gone, the new is here!" *2 Corinthians 5:17.*

COMING THROUGH LOUD AND CLEAR

The teacher handed Emma a note. Emma read it, turned to Bri, and whispered into her ear, "Cantaloupes taste good as a snack or with ice cream for dessert." Bri laughed and passed the message to Ethan. Ethan whispered it to Noah and on down the line the words were passed. At the end of the line, Jack received the message.

"So what did I write on the note?" the teacher asked.

"That's easy," Jack said with a smile. "Antelopes race good at a track or scream in the desert."

The class busted up with laughter.

"See," the teacher said. "The telephone game shows us why we can't trust stories that are passed down from person to person. We have to go to the original source."

Maybe you've heard this same argument against the Bible. Some people say the four Gospels were written so many years after Jesus' death (roughly 30 to 60 years later) that they can't be accurate. Just like with the telephone game, the message probably got garbled. That sounds possible, right?

EXAMINE THE CASE

Biblical scholar Craig A. Evans disagrees. "Unlike the telephone game, this is a community effort," he says about the writing of the Gospels. "It's not one guy who tells it to one other guy, who weeks later tells it to one other person, so that with the passage of time there would be distortion." Instead, the stories of Jesus' life were a living tradition that the community discussed. People constantly talked about what Jesus did because it was precious to them. They lived by his actions and words.

Because the Christian community guarded and cherished the stories that surrounded Jesus' life, many scholars agree that the Gospels accurately report the essential elements of Jesus' teaching, life, death, and resurrection. The Gospel of Mark, which was written around AD 60, circulated among followers of Christ who witnessed his life firsthand. If there were any errors, they would have pointed them out. During the years that many New Testament books were written, people were still alive who heard Jesus speak and watched his miracles. They knew the original material and made sure it was recorded properly. The gospel message wasn't distorted. It was reported accurately and with great detail.

The book of Proverbs tells us, "Every word of God is flawless." As you read the Bible, that's a message that comes through loud and clear.

FINAL WORD

"Every word of God is flawless" *Proverbs 30:5.*

A GOOD MEMORY

To say Nelson Dellis has a *good* memory is like saying LeBron James is *good* at basketball. Mere words don't do him justice. As a United States Memory Champion, Dellis can correctly memorize the order of a deck of fifty-two cards in less than a minute. In five minutes, he can memorize a number that's nearly 250 digits long. His memory is so good that Dellis can walk into a roomful of people and remember all of their names after just one greeting.

That's pretty amazing, especially for a guy who admits to being born with an average memory. So what changed? He did. Dellis became interested in techniques to improve his memory and then worked really hard. When he prepares for memory competitions, he'll train for five hours a day to get his mind super sharp. Dellis believes everybody can build up their memory—they just need the right techniques and plenty of determination.

EXAMINE THE CASE

In Bible times, children were really good at memorization. They had to be. Computers, books, and smartphones didn't exist. When Jewish boys were six years old, they'd go to school and begin memorizing the first five books of the Scriptures—Genesis, Exodus, Leviticus, Numbers, and Deuteronomy. By age ten, they'd know every word. The best students continued memorizing all the way to Malachi.

Some critics of the Bible say the Gospels contain legends and exaggerations, because nobody could accurately memorize everything Jesus did. After all, nearly thirty years went by before somebody wrote an account. New Testament expert Craig Blomberg wholeheartedly disagrees. "Rabbis became famous for having the entire Old Testament committed to memory," he said. "So it would have been well within the capability of Jesus' disciples to have committed much more to memory than appears in all four Gospels put together—and to have passed it along accurately."

The stories of Jesus are accurate. They give us a glimpse of everything Jesus did on earth. In fact, he did a lot more. The disciple John wrote, "Jesus did many other things as well. If every one of them were written down, I suppose that even the whole world would not have room for the books that would be written" (John 21:25). When you read the Gospels, you're getting an account of the most amazing person who ever lived. And that's worth remembering.

FINAL WORD

"Jesus did many other things as well. If every one of them were written down, I suppose that even the whole world would not have room for the books that would be written" *John 21:25*.

READ THE FINE PRINT

Have you ever taken a close look at the fine print on product labels? The label on a popular hair dryer warns not to use it while you're sleeping. If you buy the tiny iPod shuffle, the fine print says: "Do not eat iPod shuffle." (Come to think of it, it *does* look like a colorful piece of Chex cereal.) The label on a child-sized Superman costume points out, "Wearing of this garment does not enable you to fly." It may, however, give you the power to get free candy from your neighbors. The label on the classic toy Silly Putty instructs, "Do not use as ear plugs."

While the warnings on these products aren't very helpful, it's still a good idea to always read the fine print— especially in God's Word. You may have noticed instances where a reference in the text is explained at the bottom of the page. Maybe it provides the historical context of a passage or highlights where you can find similar verses. But there are several places—particularly Mark 16:9–20 and John 7:53–8:11—where the fine print lets you know that these verses weren't included in the oldest and most reliable manuscripts.

EXAMINE THE CASE

So why are those passages included in the Bible if they weren't part of the earliest texts that we have? That's the question many Bible critics ask. One critic even wrote a book, and many Christians were shocked to learn that the story of Jesus writing in the dirt and saying, "Let any one of you who is without sin be the first to throw a stone" (John 8:7), wasn't part of John's original Gospel. That was inserted later and eventually made it into modern Bibles. Discovering that fact had some people doubting the validity of God's Word. But it was never a secret that those passages weren't in the oldest and most reliable manuscripts—that fact was always in the fine print.

As you read the Bible, make sure to study it like you would a history book before a test. It can stand up to your scrutiny, because it is God's words ... not human words (1 Thessalonians 2:13). Read the fine print, because it can give you some important information.

FINAL WORD

"We also thank God continually because, when you received the word of God, which you heard from us, you accepted it not as a human word, but as it actually is, the word of God" *1 Thessalonians 2:13.*

IN GOD
WE TRUST

How *did I let my dad talk me into this?* Jessie thought as the two of them were slowly raised nearly 100 feet into the air. Her family was on a vacation in Colorado, and her dad wanted to try the Royal Rush Skycoaster—the scariest skycoaster in the world. It's not the 100-foot tower that makes this particular skycoaster scary; it's what you swing over … total nothingness.

The Royal Rush is perched on the edge of the Royal Gorge. The Arkansas River rushes by more than 1,200 feet below. (That's as tall as the Empire State Building.)

"I've never been afraid of heights until now," Jessie said.

"There's nothing to worry about," Dad answered. "This is a strong, steel cable. We've got to trust the cable."

Great, Jessie thought. *My life is in the hands of a cable.*

Slowly, they inched higher and higher above the canyon rim.

"Do you want to pull the cord?" Dad asked.

"You do it," Jessie said, her eyes squeezed shut in fear.

"Three, two, one. Let's fly!" Dad shouted as he pulled the cord.

Jessie and her dad zoomed toward the ground at nearly fifty miles per hour. She was too scared to scream as she flew over the side of the gorge. Pausing for a moment at the end of the cable, they soared back the other way.

"Yeah, this is great!" Jessie yelled as they swung back and forth. "Let's get Mom to try!"

EX AMINE THE CASE

Who do you trust with your life? Jessie trusted the cable. As Christians, we have to trust Jesus. God's Son said he came so we could have a fulfilling life (John 10:10). A lot of people say they trust God, but they don't demonstrate it with their actions. Just like Jessie, they're afraid to take a risk and pull the cord. The prophet Isaiah had some advice for Jessie and everyone: "God is my salvation; I will trust and not be afraid."

Jessie and her dad couldn't go anywhere until they trusted the steel cable. It's the same way with our faith in Christ. We're stuck until we trust him and soar into the life he has planned for us. Is there something you've wanted to do for God but have been too afraid to try? Pull the cord, trust him, and discover the amazing adventure that awaits!

FINAL WORD

"Surely God is my salvation; I will trust and not be afraid. The Lord, the Lord himself, is my strength" *Isaiah 12:2.*

THE GREATEST STORY EVER TOLD

What's your favorite Bible story?

God's Word tells amazing stories of men and women who displayed great faith. A lot of kids love Noah. Then there's Moses and the burning bush. Queen Esther saved her people by showing a lot of courage. And when it comes to courage, few displayed more than Daniel.

Taken into captivity by the Babylonians as a teenager, Daniel never stopped serving God. He followed God's rules about eating the right foods (Daniel 1). Daniel turned to God for wisdom to interpret King Nebuchadnezzar's dream (Daniel 2). He refused to stop praying to God (Daniel 6). Because he went against King Darius's command, Daniel was thrown into the lions' den. You know what happened next: Daniel walked out of the den without a scratch, and Darius praised the one true God.

In the final few chapters of Daniel, the prophet records visions about the future. Daniel 7:13–14 says, "I saw someone like a son of man coming with the clouds of heaven. He was given authority, honor, and sovereignty over all the nations of the world, so that people of every race and nation and language would obey him. His rule is eternal—it will never end" (NLT).

EXAMINE THE CASE

Did you notice the words "son of man"? Numerous times in the first three gospels, Jesus refers to himself as the "Son of Man." In Matthew 20:28 Jesus says, "For even the Son of Man came not to be served but to serve others and to give his life as a ransom for many" (NLT).

Some bestselling books have claimed that as a "son of man," Jesus was a frail human who would suffer and die. At first glance, that appears to be a good explanation. But in actuality, the term has the exact opposite meaning. By calling himself the "Son of Man," biblical experts say Jesus was referring back to the prophet Daniel, who prophesied that God's Son would come to rule over the world forever. "Son of man" wasn't a term of weakness, but of divinity. Jesus was all-powerful, yet he came to serve and die for our sins. When he rose from the dead, he set the stage for his second coming when he'll rule as a conquering king. And that's the greatest story ever.

FINAL WORD

"For even the Son of Man came not to be served but to serve others and to give his life as a ransom for many" *Matthew 20:28 NLT.*

FOLLOW HIS EXAMPLE

Does your family go to church?

Of course, you might think. *I'm reading this book, aren't I? Doesn't that show I'm serious about my faith?*

While it may seem obvious to you that followers of Jesus want to attend church, research shows that's not always the case. Four out of five American adults call themselves Christians, but only about one out of five attends church on Sundays. Some say they're too busy. Others had a bad experience and don't want to go back.

Bestselling Christian author Max Lucado has often said, "God loves you just the way you are, but he refuses to leave you that way." Part of growing as a Christian means acting more like Jesus. If we accept God's forgiveness and don't change, then something's wrong. Becoming more Christlike takes time, understanding, and encouragement. Some transformation can be worked out on your own through Bible study and prayer. But a key component of true life change comes only through church. Our journey to become more like Jesus goes better when we learn from a godly pastor and build relationships with other Christians.

EXAMINE THE CASE

If you attend church as a child, you'll probably go to church as an adult. It's not automatic, but studies show it's more likely. Numerous times in God's Word we're instructed to gather with other believers. It benefits us and is also good for God's body. And if you need another reason to attend church, then remember that Jesus went to worship services. You follow his example every time you go to youth group. Luke 4:16 tells us, "[Jesus] went to Nazareth, where he had been brought up, and on the Sabbath day he went into the synagogue, as was his custom."

Notice the words "as was his custom." It was Jesus' habit to be in God's house with other believers. And it wasn't like he *had* to. Jesus understood everything about God and his Word. He wasn't going to hear anything he didn't already know. Still, he made a point to go to church. We should do the same. And we shouldn't simply do it out of obedience. We ought to attend church with anticipation, expecting that it will change us to be more like Jesus. This week before you go to church, ask God to show you something new during the service. When you prepare your heart before stepping into God's house, you may discover something unexpected.

FINAL WORD

"[Jesus] went to Nazareth, where he had been brought up, and on the Sabbath day he went into the synagogue, as was his custom" *Luke 4:16.*

THROUGH GOD'S EYES

Pimples, zits, spots, acne. Whatever you call them, blemishes aren't fun. If you don't have them now, you'll deal with them soon enough. Medical studies show more than 80 percent of teenagers get acne at some point. Doctors say the best ways to prevent pimples are washing your face twice a day with mild soap and warm water, refraining from touching your face, keeping your hair clean, and removing makeup before going to bed. But even if you do all of those things, chances are you'll wake up one morning, stumble to the mirror, and find a huge zit on your chin. As you grow, you might not always be happy with the image you see in the mirror.

Do you ever wonder how God sees you? Even before you knew him, God loved you and wanted a relationship with you. But your sins got in the way. Your selfish thoughts, lying tongue, and jealous eyes kept you from a one-on-one connection. Once you prayed to accept Jesus as your Savior, however, God's view of you changed. He no longer saw your sins. Instead, he looked at you under a perfect covering of Jesus' grace and forgiveness.

EXAMINE THE CASE

Think about this fact: As followers of Jesus, we're seen as blameless before a perfectly holy God. That's amazing! Colossians 1:22 explains it this way: "But now he has reconciled you by Christ's physical body through death to present you holy in his sight, without blemish and free from accusation."

Even if our faces are covered with zits, God sees us as blemish-free and forgiven.

Sadly, many Christians don't live that way. We live timid lives filled with guilt from past mistakes. We see ourselves clothed in dirty rags, instead of a white robe of Jesus' righteousness. Until we embrace God's view of us, we'll never live the bold lives he has planned. Sure, we'll still make mistakes. We can never live up to God's standard. But becoming more like Christ has little to do with overcoming mistakes. It means learning from our mistakes, tapping into God's power, and trying to act as God would want us to in every situation. Live differently. Hate what God hates. Love what he loves. Strive to live a holy and blameless life. That's how God sees you. And that's who you really are!

FINAL WORD

"But now he has reconciled you by Christ's physical body through death to present you holy in his sight, without blemish and free from accusation" *Colossians 1:22*.

ON TARGET

Matt Emmons slowly exhaled as he focused on the target more than fifty yards away. After shooting 129 shots in the three-position rifle final at the 2004 Summer Olympics, he sat in first place. Matt needed just one more decent shot to win gold. He locked in on the bull's-eye, pulled the trigger, and saw the shot strike just outside the center circle. The gold medal was his!

The twenty-three-year-old looked at the scoreboard. Something was wrong. His score didn't show up. He saw the officials huddling. After a brief meeting, one of them walked over and said he'd hit the wrong target. Matt was competing in lane two, but the shot hit the target in lane three. By missing the final target, Matt received zero points and dropped from first to eighth place.

Matt had competed in shooting since he was fourteen. He knew the rules and was a great shot. He had grown up hunting with his family, and the three-position rifle competition allowed him to show his shooting skills lying down, kneeling, and standing up. Matt learned to first set his sights on the target number and then lower his gaze to the bull's-eye before firing. But on the most important shot in the Olympics, his aim was perfect but on the wrong target.

EXAMINE THE CASE

How could somebody that smart and skilled hit the wrong target? It seems impossible, right? Sadly, a lot of smart people live their lives aimed at the wrong target. Instead of focusing on God and hitting his target, they aim at a different target. Increasingly, people trust their feelings or an Internet search when it comes to spiritual beliefs. A CBS poll found nearly four out of ten people say the search for spirituality—no matter where it takes them—is more important than sticking with the traditions of the church. That's a dangerous thought.

Many church traditions are based on the Bible. And the Bible says to look to Jesus for guidance. Being sincere about your search for spiritual truth is important. But a lot of people are sincerely misguided. They may hit the target, but if it's the wrong target, it counts for nothing. Make sure you're aimed at the right target—Jesus Christ—as you make decisions about how to live your life.

FINAL WORD

"Let us keep looking to Jesus. He is the author of faith. He also makes it perfect. He paid no attention to the shame of the cross. He suffered there because of the joy he was looking forward to" *Hebrews 12:2 NIrV.*

TRUTH WINS

Barrett couldn't wait to buy the new FunStation IV video game console. It featured interactive 3-D controls, WiFi connectivity, and the newest virtual-reality gaming capabilities. Plus, it came with the latest Verminoids video game—"Avoid the Noid III." Just one problem. Everybody else wanted it too. Before the FunStation arrived in stores, lines formed weeks in advance. At first, the advertised price was $299. But with limited quantities and a huge demand, stores started charging over $500.

It's not fair, Barrett thought. *Just because everybody wants the FunStation IV, the price is skyrocketing.*

Actually, what Barrett experienced is totally fair. It's part of living in a free market economy based on supply and demand. If a product comes out that nobody desires, the price goes down and the product fails. But if everybody wants something with a limited supply, then the price goes up. Way up.

You live in a free market—not only in the economy, but also in the world of ideas. Philosophers have long believed in a "marketplace of ideas," where everybody can express their views, but only the best ideas survive.

EXAMINE THE CASE

The truth will *always* rise to the top. Unfortunately, because of the Internet, bad ideas often survive, too, because nobody goes back to take down inaccurate posts. It's up to you to find what's right. King Solomon, one of the wisest men to ever live, wrote, "I saw that wisdom is better than folly, just as light is better than darkness" (Ecclesiastes 2:13).

Edwin Yamauchi knows a lot about God's light. He has studied twenty-two languages and written over fifteen books. Born into a Buddhist family, Yamauchi prayed to accept Christ at age fifteen. In a swirling marketplace of ideas, Yamauchi warns people about articles they find on the Web.

"Even though the Internet is a quick and convenient source of information, it also perpetuates outdated and disproved theories," he said. "Check the credentials of the authors. Do they have the training and depth of knowledge to write authoritatively on these issues? Finally, be aware of the biases of many modern authors, who may clearly have an axe to grind."

That axe is often wielded at traditional Christianity. Writers on the Internet chop at the truth using weak, outdated ideas. Nearly anyone can post their opinion on the Internet whether it's right or wrong. Nobody fact-checks the validity and accuracy of many of the claims against traditional Christianity. When it comes to your belief in Christ, seek the truth from credible sources. Don't believe everything you read on the Web. By being wise, you're sure to win in the end.

FINAL WORD

"I saw that wisdom is better than folly, just as light is better than darkness" *Ecclesiastes 2:13*.

JUST FOR YOU

Shoes can be cool. Really cool. Popular shoemakers allow you to customize every detail on their website. You start by selecting the outside shoe material. Pick the color. Choose the tip and heel setup. Then search through midsole and strap colors. After picking your lining and laces, you can write a personalized message to appear on the tongue of your shoes. Just one more click and your shoes will be created according to your exact specifications.

Sixty years ago, if you wanted an athletic shoe, your choices were limited. Converse All-Stars were popular, along with Spalding and Adidas. Color choices were even narrower, unless you liked white. Today you can customize bright, technologically advanced footwear to fit your personality. And it's not just shoes that can be tweaked any way you like. Book companies allow parents or grandparents to inject a child's name into a story. Toy companies will let you create a teddy bear with a baby's name stitched into it. Whatever you want can be made just for you. Don't you feel special?

EXAMINE THE CASE

We live in a mix-and-match world. From sub sandwiches to dolls to religion, people want to pick and choose what makes them feel good. They may like the Jesus who hugged children and walked on water. But the Jesus who said to have faith and follow him makes them uncomfortable. They embrace the "soft" Jesus and combine that belief with other religions. The blending of different religions is called *syncretism*. And that's a bad idea.

Being able to customize your beliefs, like putting together a plate of food at a massive buffet, sounds enticing. But it will leave a bad taste in your mouth. The Bible teaches there is only one way—God's way. After Jesus was crucified and rose from the dead, his disciples traveled around telling people the good news. In Acts 4 Peter and John appear before the religious leaders who ask, "By what name did you do this?" Peter answers plainly. He explains that Jesus is the cornerstone of true faith and declares, "Salvation is found in no one else, for there is no other name under heaven given to mankind by which we must be saved" (Acts 4:12).

Picking and choosing can be fun when it comes to shoes, but when it comes to your beliefs, only one choice is right. And that's Jesus Christ.

FINAL WORD

"Salvation is found in no one else, for there is no other name under heaven given to mankind by which we must be saved" *Acts 4:12*.

OH, BROTHER

What is it about brothers in the Bible? If you want to know how to treat your siblings, it's hard to find good examples in there—especially the Old Testament. Jacob deceived his brother, Esau, to take all of his rights as the firstborn. Then Jacob tricked their father to receive the blessing that was meant for Esau. Joseph told his older brothers about dreams in which they all worshiped him. (Not exactly a great way to make friends.) His brothers reacted by tossing Joseph in a pit, selling him into slavery, and telling their father that a wild animal killed Joseph. And how about those first two brothers, Cain and Abel? Cain's jealously and anger took over and caused him to kill his brother. *Yikes!*

Things don't get much better in the New Testament. Jesus had several half brothers and sisters. His brothers James, Joses, Simon, and Judas are mentioned in the Bible. But according to John 7:5, "Even his own brothers did not believe in him." How could that be? By growing up with Jesus, they would've seen he was different. But maybe it was too much for them to believe that their brother was God's Son.

EXAMINE THE CASE

Wait a minute! you might be thinking. *Didn't Jesus' brother James write a book in the Bible?* Yes, he did. But he didn't believe Jesus' claims until after Jesus died. Once Jesus rose from the dead, he appeared before James to tell his brother the good news (1 Corinthians 15:7). After seeing his older brother face-to-face, James became one of Jesus' most committed followers. He was a leader in the church at Jerusalem. Some experts say James' change of heart is one of the strongest arguments for the resurrection of Jesus Christ. His encounter with the risen Jesus affected James so much that he devoted the rest of his life to telling the world the truth about his older brother, God's Son, Jesus Christ. In the end, he was put to death for his message.

The beginning of the book of James tells us to ask God for wisdom (James 1:5). As you build your case for Christ, you're going to need plenty of wisdom to sort through arguments and find the truth. Pray to God for wisdom. He'll help you find the truth—just like he did for James.

FINAL WORD

"If any of you lacks wisdom, you should ask God, who gives generously to all without finding fault, and it will be given to you" *James 1:5*.

GOING WORLDWIDE

● Hablas español?

¿With much of South and Central America, not to mention Spain, Spanish is one of the most spoken languages on the planet. English also ranks near the top. Many countries teach English in school, even if it's not their official language. But the most popular language by far is Mandarin Chinese. Some experts estimate more than 1 billion people speak Mandarin.

Linguists have a difficult time figuring out how many languages are spoken around the world. The best estimates say around 6,800 different languages exist. In the United States, nearly all 300-plus million people speak English. But in the tiny country of Papua New Guinea, there are fewer than 5.5 million people, yet they speak nearly 830 different languages!

Language is important. Without it, we wouldn't be able to communicate. Remember the story of the Tower of Babel in the Old Testament? Their project seemed to be going well until the Lord "confused their language" (Genesis 11:7). Then everything fell apart.

EXAMINE THE CASE

The Bible is clear that God wants all people to know him. For people to understand the truth about God's love, they must hear God's Word. Romans 10:17 says, "So faith comes from hearing, that is, hearing the Good News about Christ" (NLT). According to Wycliffe Bible Translators, parts of God's Word have been translated into 2,800 languages. More than 500 languages have the complete Bible. Another 1,275 feature the New Testament. Over 1,000 have at least one book already translated. Wycliffe says an additional 1,500 languages are actively being worked on so they'll have God's Word. That's a lot of work! Take a minute right now to pray and ask God to bless and give wisdom to the thousands of people who work tirelessly to translate God's Word so that his message can be known worldwide.

Translating the Scriptures into different languages is nothing new. New Testament expert Bruce Metzger says, "In addition to Greek manuscripts, we also have translations of the gospels into other languages at a relatively early time—into Latin, Syriac, and Coptic." Beyond that, the Gospels were quickly translated into Armenian, Gothic, Georgian, and Ethiopic. Not only does this show that God's Word spread quickly after Jesus died and rose from the dead, but it also helps prove the accuracy of the New Testament. With so many copies in so many languages, experts have confidence that the essential message has stayed the same over time.

FINAL WORD

"So faith comes from hearing, that is, hearing the Good News about Christ" *Romans 10:17 NLT.*

SEEK HIS FACE

They start with the hair and general face shape. From there, police sketch artists focus in on different details of a person's eyes, lips, nose, and chin. Ever since Scotland Yard first turned a witness's memory of a suspect into a facial sketch in 1889, forensic artists (that's the official term) have played an important role in law enforcement.

According to *Guinness World Records*, no artist has helped catch more criminals than Lois Gibson. For more than thirty years, Gibson has used her artistic talents to help Texas police apprehend more than 520 criminals and solve over 1,000 crimes. Before teaming up with the police, Gibson drew portraits of tourists on San Antonio's River Walk. After moving to Houston, Gibson volunteered to help draw sketches for the police. Her first two sketches didn't result in any captures, but her third drawing helped bring a criminal to justice. Seven years later, she started working full-time for the police, traveling around Texas and even different parts of the country. Gibson carries around forty pounds of equipment to do a sketch, including pastel paints, stencils, and catalogs with pictures of hundreds of noses, eyes, eyebrows, and lips. Normally, it takes her about an hour to draw a usable sketch.

EXAMINE THE CASE

Just like a sketch artist puts together details to create an image of a person's face, the Old Testament provides numerous details that help us see God's face. God is described as loving, holy, righteous, wise, and just. He's called the Alpha and Omega, Lord, Savior, King, Judge, Light, Rock, Redeemer, Shepherd, Creator, and forgiver of sin. If you put together all of those attributes and titles, what do you get?

The answer is obvious—Jesus Christ matches the picture. When you examine Jesus closely, he matches the sketch we see of God found elsewhere in the Bible. Not only does Jesus say he is God (John 10:30), but through his actions, words, life, and resurrection, he also proves he *is* God. As God, he's the ultimate power in the universe.

In 1 Chronicles 16:11 King David says, "Look to the Lord and his strength; seek his face always." When we seek the Lord's face with the same attention to detail as a sketch artist, not only will we find a living, loving God, but we'll also discover a huge source of strength.

FINAL WORD

"Look to the Lord and his strength; seek his face always"
1 Chronicles 16:11.

WHAT ARE THE CHANCES?

Who likes math? (Did somebody just groan?) While some kids love this subject and others just put up with it, math can be fun and helpful—even when you're talking about your faith.

Look at probability. This type of math predicts how likely something is to happen. For instance, if you flip a coin, there's a 50 percent chance that it will land on heads. The only other option is tails, which also comes up half of the time.

Now think about this: If you put four red marbles and one blue marble in a bag, what are the chances that you could reach in and pull out the blue marble? Well, because there are five marbles but you're looking for a specific one, you'd have one in five odds of selecting the blue marble—or about a 20 percent chance.

So what does this have to do with my faith in Christ? you ask.

A lot. Jesus didn't just show up on earth and start proclaiming he was the Messiah, sent from God. Anybody could do that. Jesus had facts to back up his claim ... lots of them. Bible experts have calculated that Jesus' life fulfilled more than 300 prophecies from the Old Testament. These prophecies (made hundreds and even thousands of years before

Jesus' birth) predicted where Jesus would be born, that he'd be betrayed by a friend, and that he'd be in the family line of king David—to name just a few.

EXAMINE THE CASE

Fulfilling over 300 prophecies sounds amazing. But to understand how awesome it is, you have to look at the probability. A science professor at a Christian college studied the chances of one man fulfilling just *eight* prophecies. He concluded the odds were one in 100,000,000,000,000,000! It just couldn't happen by chance.

Think of it this way. Imagine the state of Texas covered two feet deep in silver dollars. One is marked with an X. You're blindfolded and placed on the Oklahoma-Texas border. You can walk anywhere, but can reach down and pick up only one coin. You'd have the same chances of getting the right one as Jesus did in fulfilling eight prophecies—and he fulfilled over 300 of them! From the time he was born, angels declared, "He is the Messiah, the Lord." When you believe Jesus is God's Son, it's not blind faith. It's built on facts ... because Jesus proved who he was.

FINAL WORD

"Today in the town of David a Savior has been born to you; he is the Messiah, the Lord" *Luke 2:11*.

ORIGINAL SUPERHERO

Do you have a favorite superhero? If you asked twenty people, Superman would probably come out on top. What's not to like about the Man of Steel? He's faster than a speeding bullet, stronger than a locomotive, and able to fly around the world at supersonic speed. He's about as all-powerful as you can get. Nothing can hurt him ... well, except for kryptonite. He has X-ray vision, a Boy Scout mentality for doing good, and hair that never seems out of place (even when he's flying). Plus, his motto can't be beat: "Truth, justice, and the American way."

But there's even more to love. He was sent to earth from a far-off world by his father to save mankind. His earthly parents, Mary and Joseph*, did their best to raise him, but they always knew he had a special destiny to fulfill. When the world needed him most, he left his home, struggled alone in the wilderness, and began his public service at age thirty.

*Superman's parents are best known as John and Martha Kent. However, Martha's original name was Mary. John's middle name has always been Joseph.

Hold up! you may be thinking. *That sounds like Jesus,*

not Superman. And you're right. Since the 1930s, many characteristics of Jesus Christ have been incorporated into the red-caped wonder. Even Superman's real name, Jor-El, has significance, because *El* is the Hebrew word for God.

EXAMINE THE CASE

When it comes to superheroes, Bible expert Paul Copan believes the best place to look is at the original source: Jesus Christ. "He's no less than God incarnate," Copan says. "God breaks into the world with Jesus. He conquers sin, Satan, and death through Jesus ... If you want a spectacular Jesus, or a hero for the ages, or a Jesus who shatters all expectations and pours out love beyond comprehension—*there* he is!" Simply put, the greatest superhero of all time comes to life in the pages of the Bible.

During one of Jesus' first miracles, he heals a man who couldn't walk. Just before the healing, Jesus says, "I want you to know that the Son of Man has authority on earth to forgive sins" (Matthew 9:6). Superman may have defeated Lex Luthor (which, when you say it really fast, sounds like Lucifer), but Jesus conquered Satan and death and offers forgiveness from sins. Who do you think is more super?

FINAL WORD

"But I want you to know that the Son of Man has authority on earth to forgive sins" *Matthew 9:6.*

SOMETHING TO LAUGH ABOUT

Why do eagles like to go to church?
Because they are birds of *prey*.

What is a bee's favorite Bible verse?
Acts 16:31: "Bee-lieve in the Lord Jesus, and you will be saved."

What kind of car did the disciples drive?
A Honda. The Bible says they were all in one Accord.

Which book of the Bible gets hurt the most?
He-bruise.

What did Noah tell his sons when they went fishing?
"Easy on the bait, boys. We only have two worms."

Did you laugh at any of those jokes? Hopefully one of them tickled your funny bone, because laughing is good for you. Studies show laughter makes you healthier by boosting your immune system and reducing stress. Plus, it makes you smarter by increasing oxygen to your brain. Research indicates that when teachers use humor in their lessons, students retain more information and do better on tests. Laughter also makes you more alert and creative, because it engages both sides of your brain.

EXAMINE THE CASE

God wants us to laugh. Our joy should be contagious. Unfortunately, many people picture Christians as gloomy folks who always frown and never laugh. But that's not the picture we get in the Bible. Jesus had a great sense of humor. He probably didn't tell any knock-knock jokes, but the Gospels show he was funny.

In Luke 11, as Jesus teaches about prayer and giving, he asks the disciples a couple of questions: "Which of you fathers, if your son asks for a fish, will give him a snake instead? Or if he asks for an egg, will give him a scorpion?" (verses 11–12). Read that again. That's funny! Just picture your dad handing you a scorpion for breakfast when you asked for eggs. Jesus could've easily made his point by saying if earthly fathers know how to give good gifts to their children, just imagine the amazing gifts your heavenly Father will give you if you ask. But he didn't do that. He used a silly scene to drive home his message.

Jesus was clever. He made people laugh. So don't be afraid to laugh—even at church ... just make sure it's at the appropriate times.

FINAL WORD

"Our mouths were filled with laughter, our tongues with songs of joy. Then it was said among the nations, 'The Lord has done great things for them'" *Psalm 126:2.*

ULTIMATE FACT ABOUT FAITH

The Bible tells the story of a father who desperately wanted his son to be healed. Jesus' disciples had tried and failed. When the Lord heard this, he asked for the boy to be brought to him. The father came to Jesus and pleaded, "If you can do anything, take pity on us and help us."

"If you can?" Jesus replied. "Everything is possible for one who believes."

The boy's father exclaimed, "I do believe; help me overcome my unbelief!"

Immediately, Jesus healed the boy.

> But it's not about muster — it's about mustard.

Do you think the boy was healed because of the strength of the father's faith? No. Obviously, the father had little faith. He wanted to believe, but he had been disappointed so many times that he had difficulty believing. Now the father had faith in the right person—Jesus Christ. The ultimate truth is this: faith is only as good as the one in whom it's invested.

EXAMINE THE CASE

Jesus said, "If you have faith as small as a mustard seed, you can say to this mountain, 'Move from here to there,' and it will move. Nothing will be impossible for you" (Matthew 17:20). Nothing will be impossible for us, because nothing is impossible for God. Through God's power, our little faith can accomplish big things.

Do you have the faith to move mountains? Mountains are big. Sometimes we feel strong in our faith. Other times our faith feels pretty small. Here's the good news: It's not up to our faith to move mountains, because we have nothing to do with it. God does. He made the mountains, and only he moves them. At times, we can feel like it's up to us to muster up the faith to make something big happen. *If only I have faith, I'll get over this illness*, or *If only I have faith, I'll be able to tell that person about Jesus*. But it's not about muster—it's about mustard. Jesus said nothing is impossible for the person who has the faith of a mustard seed. Invest your tiny faith in a big God. Then trust him and see what he does. He may not always move the way we hope, but he always moves in the way that's best for us.

FINAL WORD

"Truly I tell you, if you have faith as small as a mustard seed, you can say to this mountain, 'Move from here to there,' and it will move. Nothing will be impossible for you" *Matthew 17:20.*

SOURCE OF CONFIDENCE

Alex enjoyed helping in the school library. He loved the smell of new books and the feel of crisp pages. But sometimes putting books back in the stacks got boring. One day, Alex had an idea for how to make things more exciting. As he reshelved books in the fiction section, he shouted, "Mouse! Mouse!"

All the students screamed and jumped on the tables. The librarian came running but couldn't find the mouse. Alex secretly laughed at their scared faces.

The next day, Alex got bored again. "Mouse, mouse!" he yelled. Again the students shrieked and jumped on their chairs.

The librarian calmly walked toward Alex and said, "Please don't shout 'mouse' unless there really is a mouse." Alex felt bad.

Later that week, Alex actually saw a mouse running around the bookshelves. "Mouse," he shouted. "There really is a mouse!"

This time, nobody moved. The librarian and all the students looked at Alex like he was a liar ... until the mouse ran across Laura's shoe.

EXAMINE THE CASE

Whenever you hear a story, it's good to evaluate the credibility of the source. In AD 180 Irenaeus, a bishop in the early church, wrote about four respected men who had an important story to tell:

- "Matthew published his own Gospel among the Hebrews."
- "Mark, the disciple and interpreter of Peter, himself handed down to us in writing the substance of Peter's preaching."
- "Luke, the follower of Paul, set down in a book the Gospel preached by his teacher."
- "John ... himself produced his Gospel while he was living at Ephesus in Asia."

Matthew and John were eyewitnesses to what Jesus said and did. And Mark based his writings on the testimony of one of Jesus' closest friends, Peter.

Many experts believe Mark's Gospel was written within thirty years after Jesus' death and resurrection. Luke and Matthew certainly knew about Mark's Gospel as they wrote theirs. John's Gospel came last. Although each book tells about Jesus' life, death, and resurrection, the author's unique perspective and personality show in the writing. So does their attention to detail. Luke even mentions at the beginning of his book how carefully he researched the truth (Luke 1:3). When it comes to what you read about Jesus' life in the Bible, you won't find anybody shouting "mouse." All you're going to find is gospel truth.

FINAL WORD

"Since I myself have carefully investigated everything from the beginning, I too decided to write an orderly account for you" *Luke 1:3*.

MOST EMBARRASSING MOMENT

Riley wished she could slither under the stands and disappear. Seconds before she was holding her favorite grape-flavored slushie and cheering on her school's football team. Now slushie covered her head ... and several of her friends.

"What were you thinking?" Mia yelled. "I'm covered in purple goo."

"This is never coming out of my shirt," Natalie added. "My mom's going to be *sooo* mad."

"I'm sorry," Riley whimpered, almost too embarrassed to speak. "When that bee flew at my hair, I just jerked my hands up. I totally forgot I was holding a slushie."

"Well, with all that sugar in your hair," Mia said, "bees are going to love you now."

Have you ever had something totally embarrassing happen to you? Maybe you spilled your drink at lunch, ran the wrong way on the soccer field, or forgot your lines during a play. Those are the moments you'd love to forget. You probably wouldn't want to write them down to be remembered for thousands of years, right?

Well, the Gospels include plenty of stories that make the disciples look bad.

EXAMINE THE CASE

When people tell a story, they'll often leave out embarrassing details or things that are hard to explain. Experts call this the "cover-up test." If a story sounds too good to be true, something must be missing. But nothing's missing from the Gospels.

Just look at Mark. The disciple Peter is recognized as the source—and he looks terrible. Mark, actually all the Gospel writers, details how Peter denied Christ three times on the night of his arrest. (Talk about an embarrassing moment.) Matthew shows Peter nearly drowning when he takes his eyes off Jesus as he walks on water. Numerous places the disciples fight among each other and fail to understand Jesus' teachings.

"Here's the point," explains Craig Blomberg, one of the foremost experts on the Gospels. "If they didn't feel free to leave out stuff when it would have been convenient and helpful to do so, is it really plausible to believe that they outright added and fabricated material with no historical basis? I'd say not."

The Gospel writers were men of great integrity. Their integrity guided them, along with the inspiration of the Holy Spirit, as they recorded the events of Jesus' life. The Gospels reflect their honesty in telling the whole story, even when it made them look bad. That's why you can trust the Gospels and why they've stood the test of time.

FINAL WORD

"The integrity of the upright guides them, but the unfaithful are destroyed by their duplicity" *Proverbs 11:3.*

HUMBLE HERO

New York Yankees pitcher Mariano Rivera made his career getting the hardest three outs in baseball—the last three. Rivera set more than twenty-five pitching records, including becoming the all-time saves leader. A pitcher earns a save by clinching a victory after throwing at least one inning with his team ahead by no more than three runs. In other words, every time Rivera stepped on the mound, it was a pressure-packed situation.

Rivera notched his record 602nd save on September 19, 2011, against the Minnesota Twins. After the game, instead of bragging about his accomplishment, Rivera did what he'd always done—focused on his teammates and God.

"The whole organization, my whole teammates have been a pillar for me," Rivera told a Fox News reporter. "I always have to talk about God, because that's the most important thing in my life. Yes, there have been bumps in the road, but God gave me the strength."

Only twenty-one pitchers in the history of baseball have tallied *half* the number of saves that Rivera has earned. When asked during an ESPN radio interview if being called the greatest closer embarrassed him, Mariano answered: "Yes, it does. It does make me uncomfortable because I don't like to talk about myself. I just want to be able to contribute as much as I can for the team. And the rest is just blessings from the Lord."

EXAMINE THE CASE

Mariano Rivera's talent and humility made him one of the most beloved baseball players of all time. Even his opponents respected him. He played the game like he lived his life, according to Philippians 2:3–4: "In humility value others above yourselves, not looking to your own interests but each of you to the interests of the others."

Jesus lived out those words, but to an even greater degree. Nobody had more to brag about than Jesus Christ. But you never heard him say, "Hey, check me out. I'm God's Son. I can walk on water." Instead of demanding to be served on earth, he made himself a servant and humbled himself on the cross to die for our sins.

Sometimes we might be tempted to brag if we ace a test, nail a game-winning shot, or get the lead in a play. At those times, remember Jesus' example and act humbly.

FINAL WORD

"In humility value others above yourselves, not looking to your own interests but each of you to the interests of the others"
Philippians 2:3–4.

HAIR-RAISING REALITY

Does anybody in your family have long hair? If so, grab a strand of it to try this experiment. All you need are: a piece of hair, clear tape, and a candy bar. Carefully tape the hair to the candy bar. Then gently lift it into the air. The hair should be strong enough to hold the candy bar without breaking.

Your hair is pretty strong. Scientists say if you weaved all the hair on your head into a rope, it'd be strong enough to lift a giraffe! Blondes have the most hair, averaging 150,000 hairs per head. Redheads tend to have the least with 90,000. (However, blondes have the thinnest hair, so it's good they have more of it.) A human hair grows about one centimeter per month. That means Diane Witt from Massachusetts has grown out her hair for a long time. She holds a modern-day record for longest hair at more than thirteen feet. Nearly everybody grows and loses hair every day. Nine out of ten hairs on your head are growing right now. The other hair is resting and will eventually fall out. Most people lose about 100 hairs per day.

EXAMINE THE CASE

Those are some hair-raising facts. Here's something even more amazing: God knows the number of hairs on your head. In Luke 12 Jesus explains to a crowd of thousands how God is actively involved in their lives. Jesus uses a sparrow, a nearly worthless bird, as an example to show the people how much God cares about his creation. If not one sparrow is forgotten, think about how much more concern God has for your life (Luke 12:6–7).

How have you seen God actively working in your life recently? Has he protected you from an injury, helped you find something that was lost, given you wisdom for a test, or allowed you to have favor in a difficult situation? Maybe you've seen God work in a family member or friend's life. God is always at work, but sometimes we can't see it unless we stop and look. Write down your own "God story" on these lines:

_____

_____

_____

_____

Now take a couple of moments to thank God for loving you so personally and caring for you so much.

FINAL WORD

"Are not five sparrows sold for two pennies? Yet not one of them is forgotten by God. Indeed, the very hairs of your head are all numbered. Don't be afraid; you are worth more than many sparrows" *Luke 12:6–7.*

HELPING OTHERS, HELPING CHRIST

Piper Hayward didn't go to Africa thinking much about clean drinking water. Her family had helped start an organization to help orphans, and the Ohio tween traveled to Kenya to do whatever she could. She even brought a trunk full of school supplies. But once Piper got to the Maasai village, she was surprised to find girls about her age who were responsible for providing water. They had no time for school, because water was scarce and took a long time to carry.

Piper enjoyed playing with the orphans, performing skits, and comforting children during medical exams. But when she returned home, she couldn't get the "water girls" out of her mind. She set up a coin drive in her school. Soon Piper's friends and family members began collecting coins in Illinois, Texas, and other states. In less than a year, enough money had been raised to drill a 600-foot well and install a pump and generator. Now the village would enjoy clean water and everybody could have a chance to go to school.

EXAMINE THE CASE

Clean water. Most of us don't think much about it. We crank the faucet and out it pours. But in many parts of the world, clean water isn't a reality. According to the World Health Organization (WHO), nearly 3.5 million people die each year from water-related diseases. A 2010 study by WHO and UNICEF discovered that 780 million people around the world don't have access to clean water. That's about one out of every nine people on the planet or more than twice the population of the United States and Canada combined!

When Piper saw a need, she worked to fix it. Anytime you reach out to help the less fortunate, you honor God and further his kingdom. In Matthew 25 Jesus tells a parable in which the king commends his true followers for helping the hungry, sick, and imprisoned, saying, "Whatever you did for one of the least of these brothers and sisters of mine, you did for me." As Christians, we know helping others is part of our role on earth. Can you think of some people who need help? You may not be providing water. But you can help the homeless in your area, volunteer in the church nursery, or use your allowance to sponsor a child in another country. Now don't just think about what you can do—go out and do it.

FINAL WORD

"The King will reply, 'Truly I tell you, whatever you did for one of the least of these brothers and sisters of mine, you did for me'" *Matthew 25:40.*

CAN YOU DIG IT?

If you've ever watched an adventure movie where the characters look for ancient treasures, it probably made the life of an archaeologist look very exciting. They get to wear cool hats, travel to exotic countries, and uncover amazing discoveries every day. But the life of most archaeologists isn't quite as thrilling.

If you want to be an archaeologist, you'd better like cleaning up because you'll do a lot of sweeping. Visit any dig site, and you'll find dozens of brooms. Stiff, black-bristled brooms work well for removing thin layers of dirt. Soft-bristled brooms brush away tiny amounts of dust without damaging a finding. Even paintbrushes are used for the most delicate work. Not only must archaeologists discover ancient artifacts, but they also have to make sure not to damage them. Hand trowels and small pickaxes dig through harder surfaces. Shovels and buckets carry away dirt. Archaeologists have multifaceted jobs, but the most important one is to carefully dig into history without sweeping away the truth.

EXAMINE THE CASE

At the beginning of the book of Luke, the author says he carefully investigated everything so he could write an orderly account of

Jesus' life. He records details about cities, leaders, and countries. Luke 3 talks about John the Baptist and mentions that Lysanias was tetrarch of Abilene. For years, some scholars pointed to this as evidence that Luke didn't know what he was talking about. They said Lysanias was a leader of Chalcis fifty years earlier. *If Luke can't get this fact right,* they suggested, *how can anything he wrote be trusted?*

But more recently, archaeologists discovered an inscription dating between AD 14 and 37 that names Lysanias as tetrarch in Abila near Damascus. It turned out there were two government officials named Lysanias, so Luke was correct! A prominent archaeologist examined Luke's references to thirty-two countries, fifty-four cities, and nine islands. His conclusion? Luke didn't make a single mistake.

"Archaeology has not produced anything that is unequivocally a contradiction to the Bible," says archeological expert John McRay.

In Luke 19 Jesus triumphantly enters Jerusalem on the back of a donkey. As his disciples shout praises, some Pharisees tell Jesus to make the people be quiet. Jesus answers, "I tell you, if they were to keep silent, the stones would cry out!" (HCSB). Today, the stones *do* cry out. And they say what we read in the Bible is true.

FINAL WORD

"He answered, 'I tell you, if they were to keep silent, the stones would cry out!'" *Luke 19:40 HCSB.*

COPYCATS

I *will not speak when the teacher is talking.*
I will not speak when the teacher is talking.
   I will not speak when the teacher is talking ...

For years teachers have punished students by having them copy sentences on the board. But if you were a scribe in the years before Jesus was born, copying words wouldn't have been a punishment but an honor.

The modern printing press was invented around 1440. That's roughly 1,400 years after Jesus was crucified. But before Jesus walked the earth, the Israelites followed God's written commands. Of course, you couldn't just go to a bookstore and pick up a copy of the Bible. Bookstores, let alone books (or the Bible), didn't exist. God's Word was painstakingly written down on scrolls. And that's where the scribes come in.

Using a reed dipped in charcoal, gum, and water, scribes carefully copied God's Word. As they wrote, they said each word out loud. Once a line was finished, they counted each letter to make sure nothing was missing or added. If a mistake was made, the scroll was taken to a guarded room until it could be destroyed.

EXAMINE THE CASE

By accurately copying the Word of God and destroying corrupted copies, the scribes ensured that the Lord's message in Isaiah 40:8 would come true: "The grass withers and the flowers fall, but the word of our God endures forever."

If a book is filled with errors, will it last for thousands of years? Probably not. It'll be revised and rewritten to correct the falsehoods. People want the truth. Lies are uncovered and discarded. The truth lasts forever. When you pick up a copy of the Bible, you can be confident that its message is true. Experts who have studied thousands of manuscripts praise the integrity with which the Bible has been transmitted over time. Not a single cardinal doctrine is in any doubt. That precision is amazing!

Take a few minutes today to act like a scribe by writing down your favorite verse ten times. If you don't have a favorite, look at these:

- Proverbs 16:3
- John 3:16
- Philippians 4:13
- Jeremiah 29:13
- Romans 12:2
- 1 Timothy 4:12

As you write, thank God for the faithful people who guarded and passed down God's Word so you can read it and memorize it today.

FINAL WORD

"The grass withers and the flowers fall, but the word of our God endures forever" *Isaiah 40:8*.

GOD RULES

Believe it or not, these laws really exist. They sound pretty silly, right? And there are plenty of funny (and obvious— after all, who'd actually strap a child to a car?) laws in states that begin with letters other than O.

In Oregon, it's illegal to strap a child to the fender or roof of an automobile. In Oklahoma, wrestling a bear could get you thrown in prison. In Ohio, you can't take a bird into a bakery.

The Bible contains some seemingly strange laws as well. Leviticus 19:19 tells us, "Do not wear clothing woven of two kinds of material." Earlier in Leviticus 13:47–50, we read that any fabrics—wool, linen, or leather—spoiled with a defiling mold "must be shown to the priest," who should examine the affected area for seven days. Why is the Bible so concerned with fashion and dirty laundry?

While some biblical laws may seem silly, God gave them to us for a specific reason. Some experts believe clothing woven from linen and wool would trap the desert heat and cause the wearer to get blisters. Others say God encouraged his people to wear "pure" fabrics as a reminder to keep themselves pure. And as far as mold goes, those infected fabrics could spread dangerous diseases, so the priests protected the people from harm. After Moses passed on God's laws, he said, "Observe them carefully, for this will show your wisdom and understanding to the nations ... What other nation is so great as to have their gods near them the way the Lord our God is near us whenever we pray to him? And what other nation is so great as to have such righteous decrees and laws?" (Deuteronomy 4:6–8). According to Moses, God's laws weren't a burden but a blessing.

EXAMINE THE CASE

When Jesus came to earth, he proclaimed the rule of God. Not only does the heavenly Father rule over everything, but he also makes all the rules. God didn't give us his commandments to boss us around and ruin our fun. His laws actually free us up. Instead of limiting our freedom, God's rules give us the freedom to live guilt-free and joyous lives.

In Deuteronomy 10:13 Moses says, "Keep the Lord's commands and statutes I am giving you today, *for your own good*" (HCSB, emphasis added). By following God's laws, you can enjoy a more powerful life. God's commands make us free to experience his love, free from the harm of making foolish choices, and free from the consequences of sin. Think about that fact the next time you're bummed out about something you can't do. God made the rules for your own good. Just like Oklahoma lawmakers prohibited bear wrestling, which would most likely land you in the hospital—let alone jail.

FINAL WORD

"Keep the Lord's commands and statutes I am giving you today, for your own good" *Deuteronomy 10:13 HCSB.*

ACT LIKE A DOG

Do you buy your pet gifts? According to the American Pet Products Association, more than 50 percent of dog owners buy their pooch a present every Christmas. Dogs, maybe more than any other pet, have a way of endearing themselves to us. They always seem so happy when we walk in the door. Tail wagging, voice barking, tongue licking—a dog's greeting can be something special.

According to the American Pet Products Association, more than 50 percent of dog owners buy their pooch a present every Christmas.

But have you ever wondered why dogs lick you? One theory is dogs lick you *because* they like you. They're showing affection. Licking is also a sign of submission. In wild dog packs, the more subordinate dogs lick the dominant ones. So when your dog licks you, it shows that you're in charge. Dogs also lick to gain information. Their keen sense of smell tells them something about who you are. It's also probably true that dogs like to lick. They get salt from your skin and licking gives them a sense of security.

EXAMINE THE CASE

That's a lot of reasons to lick, but do you believe dogs think about all that when they lick you? Probably not. They just want to show their love. We should have the same attitude when it comes to our relationship with Christ. As you read these devotions and dig into your Bible, you'll learn a lot of facts about Jesus. Maybe those facts will increase your appreciation for God. But following God is more than knowing facts—it's about showing your love.

Pastor and professor Gregory Boyd knows more facts about Jesus than most people on the planet. But he says his love for Jesus goes beyond his understanding of *facts*. "To have a relationship with Jesus Christ goes beyond just knowing the historical facts about him, yet it's rooted in the historical facts about him." Here's a fact that will only strengthen your feelings toward Christ: "This is real love—not that we loved God, but that he loved us and sent his Son as a sacrifice to take away our sins" (1 John 4:10 NLT). God loved us before we loved him. He knew the bad stuff about us and still wanted to have a relationship. When we think about Jesus, we should want to run to him in excitement—just like a dog runs to us—but we should probably refrain from licking his face.

FINAL WORD

"This is real love—not that we loved God, but that he loved us and sent his Son as a sacrifice to take away our sins" *1 John 4:10 NLT.*

THE SECRET
TO GIVING

L arry Stewart knew something about giving. But for twenty-five years, nobody knew his name. He was only known as Kansas City's Secret Santa. Stewart would simply walk up to a stranger, put $100 in their hand, smile, and say, "This is for you."

Over the course of his life, Stewart gave away well over $1 million. He often didn't have a plan for how to pass out his money. He'd go to a thrift store, the bus station, a Laundromat, or a fast-food restaurant and look for somebody in need. Then he'd go over, give some money (sometimes $1,000 at a time), and say, "God bless you." Those weren't empty words to Stewart. He knew God had blessed him, and he wanted to bless others. During a 2006 interview with *USA Today*, Stewart said before he began giving away his millions, "Part of my daily prayer was, 'Lord, lift me up and let me be a better witness to you and for you and somehow reach more people.' I had no idea this is what he had in mind."

Stewart died in 2007, but he inspired numerous others to give generously without expecting anything in return.

EX AMINE THE CASE

Part of being a follower of Jesus is giving. God has given us so much—forgiveness through his Son, a beautiful planet, family, friends, food, clothes (really every gift is from God). We reflect God's giving nature when we give to others. Plus, when we freely give, it shows we recognize God as Lord over everything we have.

Sometimes it's not easy to give. When we receive our allowance or a big check from Grandma, we might have something special we want to purchase for ourselves. But we should always give to God first. The Old Testament talks about God's people giving a *tithe*, or 10 percent of what they had, to God. But more than what we give, God cares about *how* we give. Second Corinthians 9:7 says, "Each of you should give what you have decided in your heart to give, not reluctantly or under compulsion, for God loves a cheerful giver."

Think about what you can give to God. You may not have a lot of money, but you can give your time or old toys and clothes to people in need. And as you give, make sure you do it cheerfully—that's the secret to giving.

FINAL WORD

"Each of you should give what you have decided in your heart to give, not reluctantly or under compulsion, for God loves a cheerful giver" *2 Corinthians 9:7.*

THE B-I-B-L-E— THAT'S THE BOOK FOR YOU

What's the smallest part of a word? Answer: a letter. What's the smallest part of the Bible? Answer: a letter.

Okay, that last question was a little tricky. The first thing that popped into your head was probably: *a verse*. But when the Bible was being written, it was done in books and letters—not chapters and verses.

About 800 years ago, chapters were added to the Bible. Three hundred years later, in 1551, the chapters were divided into verses. The divisions were created so it'd be easier to find specific parts of Scripture. Can you imagine saying, "My favorite sentence in the Bible is the one in Matthew that comes after the part where Jesus curses a fig tree"? It's much easier to say, "One of my favorite verses is Matthew 21:22."

Before the invention of the printing press around 1440, there weren't a lot of Bibles (let alone books). For the most part, only churches could afford to own a Bible. The people relied on priests to tell them what was in God's Word. Most Bibles were written in Latin, a language that only the well-educated could read and speak. John Wycliffe translated the Bible into English for the first time in 1382. Today, nine of ten families in the United States own a Bible. Bibles are also some of the most popular apps and get downloaded on hundreds of thousands of smartphones.

EXAMINE THE CASE

The Bible was never meant to be locked away and only listened to once a week at church. We should read and learn more from God's Word every day. The writers of the Bible knew its power. In 2 Timothy 3:16–17 you'll find these words: "All Scripture is God-breathed and is useful for teaching, rebuking, correcting and training in righteousness, so that the servant of God may be thoroughly equipped for every good work."

How often do you read the Bible for yourself? The question isn't meant to make you feel guilty. But when you have a book that contains God's inspired words for teaching, training, and equipping for good works, it's something that deserves your time. This week try to read the Bible for at least five minutes every day. You'll be amazed at what you learn.

FINAL WORD

"All Scripture is God-breathed and is useful for teaching, rebuking, correcting and training in righteousness, so that the servant of God may be thoroughly equipped for every good work" *2 Timothy 3:16–17.*

RECIPE FOR DISASTER

Olivia couldn't wait to make her grandma's famous double-chocolate delight brownies. Her family had baked this delicious treat for years. Olivia began by measuring a cup of cocoa. Then she added baking soda, melted butter, and water. Next came sugar, eggs, and flour. She stirred everything together and took a look.

Almost ready to put in the oven, Olivia thought.

She added a little salt, some vanilla extract, and chopped pecans. Then came the last ingredient—two cups of dark chocolate chips. It was perfect!

Well, almost. Gummy bears were Olivia's favorite candy. They made everything better, so she poured a bunch into the batter. Then Olivia remembered something her teacher said at school: "Protein is important for a growing body." She opened the refrigerator and found some leftover ground beef from the tacos her family ate the previous night.

Perfect, Olivia thought. *Now the brownies will be healthy, too.*

She grabbed the meat, mixed it in, and popped the brownies in the oven. Forty minutes later they were ready to serve. Olivia poured herself a tall glass of milk and cut out a huge brownie. She sat down at the table, picked up a square of piping hot, chocolaty goodness, and took a big bite.

EXAMINE THE CASE

How do you think Olivia's brownies tasted? Did the extra ingredients make them better or worse? The answer is obvious—meat brownies are disgusting!

The same thing is true about God's Word. You don't need to add anything to it to make it better. It's perfect already. In the Old Testament, Moses told God's people, "You shall not add to the word which I command you, nor take from it." The message is clear. Yet some people want to add to the Bible even today. They find other ancient texts that "fit" or put in things that God never intended to be in his Word.

During Jesus' day, the Pharisees added traditions and rules to God's Word that weren't supposed to be there. They acted holy and made a big deal of showing how much they served God. Those actions made Jesus sick (sort of like biting into a meat brownie). As you study the Bible, take God's Word at its word. If anything gets added or taken away from God's commands, it's a recipe for disaster.

FINAL WORD

"You shall not add to the word which I command you, nor take from it, that you may keep the commandments of the Lord your God" *Deuteronomy 4:2 NKJV.*

LOOK UP, NOT DOWN

Beware of "tech neck." No, this isn't a robot monster with a metal neck. It's even scarier than that. Tech neck is a medical condition created by constantly looking down at electronic devices—and it's on the rise. Doctors have also seen an increase in "text thumb," an injury caused by too much texting. Medical professionals say these kinds of repetitive-stress injuries used to be seen in people in their sixties. Now teenagers and college students are among the millions afflicted.

Physical therapists have created exercises to combat these conditions. If you feel a bout of text thumb coming on, touch your thumb to each of your fingers and repeat five times. You can also wrap a rubber band around your hand and then open it against the resistance. Many people have started to get massages to cure their tech neck. But that can be expensive. An easier solution: stop looking down!

Computer screens, cell phones, tablets. With more and more screen-based electronics, we find ourselves looking down a lot. Write a paper. Look down. Read a book on a Nook. Look down. Receive a text. Look down. Instead of looking down to communicate or find information, we need to be looking up.

EXAMINE THE CASE

When it comes to living our everyday lives, we should keep our eyes focused on God, not an electronic device. Sure, we look down when we bow our heads in prayer. But the Bible tells us to fix our eyes on Christ. Isaiah 58:11 promises, "The Lord will always lead you, satisfy you in a parched land, and strengthen your bones" (HCSB). The Lord leads us in different ways. God's commands help point us in the right direction. They give us wisdom when we have to make a tough decision. The Holy Spirit nudges us and reminds us of God's teachings on the correct way to go. And God uses people in our lives—parents, pastors, and other family members—who can provide godly advice.

When you come to a difficult situation, remember to look up to God. His way is always the right way. When we follow God's path, he gives strength to our bones—not a pain in our necks.

FINAL WORD

"The Lord will always lead you, satisfy you in a parched land, and strengthen your bones. You will be like a watered garden and like a spring whose waters never run dry" *Isaiah 58:11 HCSB.*

THE TRUTH ABOUT TRUTH

Chloe stared. Her mouth hung open. She had babysat the Miller kids before, and nothing had ever gone wrong. But after leaving the older two Miller children in the living room to check on the baby, Chloe returned to find the family's huge rubber tree lying in the middle of the white carpet. Dirt was everywhere.

"What happened?!" Chloe said, trying not to shout.

"Well," little Jack said. "A gorilla just burst into the living room and he didn't like that plant."

Do you think Jack was telling the truth? Some people will argue there is no real truth. What's true for one person may not be true for another. But professor and author Paul Copan says there is absolute truth. "People instinctively understand that truth is a belief, story, ideal, or statement that matches up with reality or corresponds to the way things really are," he explains. According to that definition, Jack probably wasn't telling the truth — unless he lived at a zoo or in western Africa.

> Some people don't like the truth, because it limits what they're able to do. They define truth as *what makes them feel good.* But that's not what the Bible says. All truth is God's truth.

EXAMINE THE CASE

Some people don't like the truth, because it limits what they're able to do. They define truth as *what makes them feel good*. But that's not what the Bible says. All truth is God's truth. In John 16:13 Jesus says a helper will come to guide us to the truth. As followers of Christ, we have the Holy Spirit to help us discern what is true. When we hear somebody telling a lie—or when we tell one ourselves—we can feel in our gut that it's wrong. The same thing is true when we're reading a book, surfing the Internet, or studying a textbook. The truth jumps out at us.

We can know what is true, because we know the Truth (John 14:6). But that doesn't mean people who don't believe the Bible are totally in the dark. Even if two people don't share all the same beliefs, they can still agree on some truths. And once you find a point of agreement with someone, you may be able to help lead them to the ultimate truth of Jesus Christ.

Take a few minutes to write three statements you know are true:

1.

2.

3.

Then thank God for sending the Holy Spirit so that you can know the whole truth.

FINAL WORD

"When he, the Spirit of truth, comes, he will guide you into all the truth" *John 16:13*.

SEND A MESSAGE

Here's a ?4U. Do you have any friends who text more than they talk? Some studies say the average teenager sends over eighty text messages a day. That's more than 3,000 a month!

Texting seems to be the way a lot of kids communicate — and they're good at it. Thirteen-year-old Morgan Pozgar won the first National Texting Championship in 2007. Since that time, teens have claimed every title, including Wisconsin's Austin Wierschke who notched back-to-back wins (and $100,000) in 2011 and 2012. Austin isn't just fast at texting — he's also accurate. To win the title in 2012, he had to text a line from "Twinkle, Twinkle, Little Star" while blindfolded and also send a phrase that was written backwards.

You probably text under less stressful circumstances (and not in front of cameras and a live audience). But accuracy is equally important in your messages. You want to make sure the correct information gets communicated. And when you hear the familiar whistle of your cell phone alerting you about an incoming text message, what do you normally find? Most likely, it's a message from a friend or family member. But sometimes you see a spam message: "Your number was selected as our iPad winner of the day! Enter 'IPAD' to redeem." Some messages are more important than others. What happens to the spam? *Delete*.

EXAMINE THE CASE

As followers of Christ, we're called to tell others about Jesus. God wants us to be his witnesses. Maybe you're afraid to spread the good news about Jesus because you feel everybody has heard it before and you don't want them to hit *delete*. But you can't give up. The case for Christ is solid and reliable. More people need to hear about it.

The book of Romans asks a good question: "How can they believe in the one of whom they have not heard? And how can they hear without someone preaching to them?" (Romans 10:14). As you text your friends, make sure you're not ignoring your faith. Tell them you're praying for them. Text an encouraging Bible verse to somebody who's down. We need to keep sending out Christ's message of love. With some persistence and creativity, the life-changing message of Jesus Christ will catch someone's eye and help bring them into God's family. Now that sounds 2G2BT (to good to be true), but it *is* true.

FINAL WORD

"How can they believe in the one of whom they have not heard? And how can they hear without someone preaching to them?" *Romans 10:14*.

LIGHT IN THE DARKNESS

Seeing a hippopotamus at a zoo can be fun. Seeing one in the wild is dangerous. Hippos kill more humans every year in Africa than any other large animal. Male hippos aggressively defend their territory in rivers. Mother hippos can become violent if they sense their babies are in danger. Despite their huge size—males grow over twelve feet long and five feet tall and weigh more than 5,000 pounds—hippos can run over 20 miles per hour.

Mary Slessor was only five feet tall and weighed around 100 pounds when she went to Africa in 1874. After growing up in Scotland with an alcoholic and abusive father, at age twenty-eight Mary followed her dream of becoming a missionary. When she arrived in Nigeria, her blue eyes and fiery red hair stood out. She cut her hair, walked around barefoot, and wore African dresses to fit in. Mary was fearless, caring, and brave. Soon she became known as "White Ma." Babies began appearing on her doorstep. Sometimes they were children their families couldn't care for. Other times they were twins, who were believed by superstitious villagers to have an evil spirit. Often twins were killed. Mary saved some. Once as she returned with twins from a village on the river, a hippopotamus charged her boat. Mary pounded the large animal on the head with a cooking kettle. When the hippo lunged again with its mouth open, Mary slammed the kettle into its jaws. *Crunch!* The hippo turned and swam away.

EXAMINE THE CASE

Mary Slessor lived an amazing life serving God in Africa. God may never call you to go to Africa, but you are called to serve. Isaiah 58:10 tells us that serving others makes us like bright lights in a dark world. Part of what made Jesus' ministry on earth so unique is that he served the oppressed. He ate with sinners. He healed untouchable lepers. His light shone brightly in the darkness. Yours can too.

You can make a big difference for God right where you are. Look around for opportunities to help the hungry or oppressed. You could be a huge help by befriending a lonely kid at school. By "spending" yourself serving others, you will be a light for God.

FINAL WORD

"If you spend yourselves in behalf of the hungry and satisfy the needs of the oppressed, then your light will rise in the darkness, and your night will become like the noonday" *Isaiah 58:10.*

BIGGEST, BEST GOD

"**O**h yeah?" Nathan yelled. "Well, my dad drives a monster truck!"

"That's nothing," Mason replied. "My dad can eat jalapeño peppers without crying."

For centuries, playground battles have been fought over the issue of whose dad is better. You may have even found yourself sticking up for your dad, saying, "My dad is the best, because he can throw a Frisbee across an entire football field."

While these arguments may seem childish, don't be surprised if you get caught in similar battles about your faith as you grow up. With so many different religions and beliefs, you could end up defending your heavenly Father by shouting, "Oh yeah, well my God is the only one to rise from the dead!"

Defending your faith is important, but it's hard to introduce other people to your loving Father when you're shouting about how your God is the biggest and best.

EXAMINE THE CASE

It's true that the God of Christianity is the one true God. The first commandment says, "You shall have no other gods before me" (Exodus 20:3). Our God is the only God deserving of our trust and worship.

At the same time, as we defend our beliefs, we should try not to come across as close-minded know-it-alls. That only turns off other people from accepting Jesus as Savior. Many of the people you meet will value tolerance above honesty, integrity, and conviction. That's a sad statement about society, but it's true. Tolerance has also seeped into the belief systems of many Christians. A survey of people who said they were Christians found that 70 percent of them thought many religions could lead to eternal life. That's just not the case!

Jesus said, "I am the way and the truth and the life. No one comes to the Father except through me" (John 14:6). We need to live with confidence, knowing that God is the only way to eternal life. As we interact with people, we should strive to show love and respect. We can't bully or argue anybody into believing the truth about God. But our words and actions can demonstrate God's love, which could lead people to understand that his way is the *only* way to go.

FINAL WORD

"Jesus answered, 'I am the way and the truth and the life. No one comes to the Father except through me'" *John 14:6.*

GETTING STRONGER ... BY RESTING

Olympic weight lifter Shane Hamman knew something about bulking up. The Oklahoma native grew up country strong. He spent hours lifting buckets of huge watermelons at his father's fruit market. As a child, Shane excelled on the soccer and football fields. But during his teen years, he discovered weight lifting. He immediately started breaking records. Over the next fifteen years, Shane competed in two Olympics (2000 and 2004), won nine national weight-lifting championships, and broke every U.S. record in the 105 (kg)-plus division. At five feet nine inches tall and 350 pounds, this strong man knew where his power came from, saying, "I realized early on my strength was a gift from God. I totally dedicated my weightlifting to him to be used for his glory."

Shane trained at the U.S. Olympic Training Center in Colorado Springs, Colorado, working with the top experts on muscle building. By properly training his body through strenuous exercise, good nutrition, and proper rest, Shane became seriously strong. He could squat more than 1,000 pounds, bench over 550, clean and jerk more than 520, and snatch 435. "Just due to the type of training, it developed me into a really good athlete," Shane said.

Try to picture a 350-pound guy pulling a backflip. Shane could do it. Plus, with a thirty-six-inch vertical leap, he could slam dunk a basketball.

EXAMINE THE CASE

Shane knew his strength came from God and that God requires us to rest. In Matthew 11 Jesus says he gives rest to the weary. "Take my yoke upon you and learn from me, for I am gentle and humble in heart, and you will find rest for your souls" (Matthew 11:29). Rest is a key component to growing stronger in your physical body and spiritual life.

Muscle building requires a balance of muscle tearing and muscle rebuilding. When you lift weights, it creates tiny tears in the muscle. These tears are needed to create new muscle. As you rest, God allows your body to repair the muscle and make it bigger. Similarly, you need time to rest and grow closer to God. By taking a sabbath—or day of rest—you can focus on your relationship with him. The Lord wants us to enjoy going to church and relaxing with him. Without recovery time, you'll just "tear" through life ... and that's not the way God intended you to live.

FINAL WORD

"Remember the Sabbath day by keeping it holy. Six days you shall labor and do all your work, but the seventh day is a sabbath to the Lord your God" *Exodus 20:8–10.*

RELATIONSHIP, NOT RELIGION

What's the first word that pops into your head when you think about Jesus? You may think: *kind, loving, God, Savior, good, powerful, mighty.* Jesus is all of those things and more. Jesus showed his kindness in many ways. He healed people from sickness. He called little children to come to him (Matthew 19:14). He fed thousands. He taught people God's truth.

While Jesus spoke with amazing kindness to nearly everybody he met, there was one group of people he spoke harshly to—the religious leaders. When Jesus walked the earth, many of the religious leaders put up a false front. They tried to look holier than everybody else, but they had hearts that were far away from God. Jesus wanted honesty instead of showiness. They were fake, and he called them on it. In Matthew 23:25 Jesus said, "Woe to you, teachers of the law and Pharisees, you hypocrites! You clean the outside of the cup and dish, but inside they are full of greed and self-indulgence." Jesus went on to say it's imperative to clean the inside of the cup first, then the outside will be clean.

EXAMINE THE CASE

Obviously, Jesus wasn't talking about "cups." He was talking about the condition of our hearts. Many of the religious leaders in Jesus' day were stuck being, well … religious. *Religion* is defined as "a system of faith and worship." They did all the "right" things by praying in public, giving money to God's work, and memorizing the Scriptures. Many Pharisees took pride in following God's laws. But being a Christian isn't about following a list of dos and don'ts. It *is* about having a relationship with Jesus Christ.

Instead of outward actions, Jesus is more concerned about our inward beliefs and purity. Saying one thing and doing another is the ultimate sign of hypocrisy. When you say you're a Christian, you need to act like one. Your actions should come from a sincere heart that wants to follow God—not from the desire of having other people look at you and say, "What a good person."

Take a minute to honestly assess your motivation for doing the right things: Is it to please God, or is it to look good to the people around you?

FINAL WORD

"Woe to you, teachers of the law and Pharisees, you hypocrites! You clean the outside of the cup and dish, but inside they are full of greed and self-indulgence" *Matthew 23:25*.

IDEAL IDOL

Sydney had a bad fever—Bieber fever, that is. She couldn't stop talking about the popular pop star. Before her Justin Bieber affliction, Sydney loved the Jo-Bros. Actually, anytime a new boy band or teen heartthrob popped up in popular culture, Sydney was the first to buy a poster and join the fan club.

Do you think Sydney had a problem? She didn't think so. She said she was just being a loyal fan and loyalty was a good thing. While loyalty is good, being obsessed with anything other than God is bad. Numerous times the Bible warns us about worshiping an idol.

But wait, you say. *I'm not building a golden calf or bowing down to a false god.* The truth is, many things can become an idol. We can become obsessed with getting good grades, wearing the right clothes, playing video games, having the coolest gadgets, being popular, or knowing the latest music. Anything that consumes our time, thoughts, money, or energy can develop into an idol in our lives.

EXAMINE THE CASE

Jesus Christ warrants our worship. First John 5:20–21 tells us, "We know also that the Son of God has come and has given us understanding, so that we may know him who is true ... Dear children, keep yourselves from idols." Absolute truth can be found only in God's Son. Anything that distracts us from our relationship with Christ can serve as an idol—even the Bible. Some Bible teachers have seen students become so amazed by God's Word that they start to worship the Bible over God. The Bible is amazing. Discovering how God protected his written word can increase our faith. But the Bible is very clear: We should worship only God. We should always worship the Creator over the created.

Think about your life. Is there anything that's taking the top spot away from God? It could be a relationship with a friend, playing sports, or performing in musicals. Write down anything that could be an idol:

• • •

Now pray to God and give that thing to him. Tell God, *I don't want anything in my life to come before you. I want to glorify you with my* (fill in the blank: sports, music, friends, etc.). *Help me to only worship you and honor you in everything I do.*

FINAL WORD

"We know also that the Son of God has come and has given us understanding, so that we may know him who is true.... Dear children, keep yourselves from idols" *1 John 5:20–21.*

BETTER THAN GOLD

Three-year-old James Hyatt didn't set out to find a $4 million gold pendant. It just happened. On a gray May day in 2010, he was walking with his dad and grandfather in a field in southwest England. James asked if he could use the metal detector. After a few minutes, it started beeping. His dad dug into the muddy soil. Only eight inches below the surface, he struck gold and pulled out a pendant. Made in the early 1500s with an image of the Virgin Mary holding a cross, the rare artifact was valued at more than $4 million!

Gold is one of the most precious metals on the planet. But when it's first mined from the ground, it contains many impurities. By heating the metal to nearly 2,000° Fahrenheit, metal experts test the gold and refine it until it's pure and extremely valuable.

EXAMINE THE CASE

Many times the Scriptures say that God's Word is worth more than gold. But like gold, the contents of the Bible had to be tested. Early church leaders looked at the writings after Jesus' death and resurrection to determine which books were authoritative and pure.

"Basically, the early church had three criteria," explains renowned New Testament scholar Bruce Metzger. First, the books must have been written by apostles, who were eyewitnesses to what they wrote about, or by followers of apostles (remember that Mark helped Peter, and Luke traveled with Paul). Second, the leaders made sure the books conformed to what was called the "rule of faith." The documents needed to align with basic Christian traditions recognized by the church. Third, the documents had to have been used and accepted by the church for many years. In other words, any strange new teachings or anything that went against Jesus' words didn't make the cut.

Within 200 years of Jesus' crucifixion, church leaders were nearly unanimous about which books should be in the New Testament. That means every book that appears in today's Bibles was put to the test. Similarly, the apostle Paul encourages all believers to scrutinize their beliefs. As followers of Christ, we need to test what we read and hear about God and only hold on to what is good (1 Thessalonians 5:20–21). That's basically what the early church did with writings about Jesus. When we hear a teaching about Christ, we need to think about it carefully. If it doesn't align with the Bible or what we know of God's character, throw it out. Only hold on to the truth.

FINAL WORD

"Do not treat prophecies with contempt but test them all; hold on to what is good" *1 Thessalonians 5:20–21*.

AGREED WITH THE CREED

Do you belong to any teams or organizations that have a creed? The term *creed* comes from a Latin word that means "I believe." The Boy Scouts have a famous creed that was written in the early 1900s by Ludvig Dale: "To be trustworthy in all things. Loyal, helpful, friendly, courteous and kind. To learn obedience and practice cheerfulness and thrift. To be brave, clean and reverent. Above all to keep myself physically strong, mentally awake and morally straight. To 'be prepared' at all times to do my duty to God and my country, and to do a good turn to someone every day." The Girl Scouts have a similar creed.

But the most famous creed ever written is the Nicene Creed, which explains the core beliefs of Christianity. Less than 300 years after Jesus' resurrection, Constantine won control over the Roman Empire. As emperor, he made Christianity the official religion. (Before this time, Christians suffered horrible persecution from Rome.) Because of different understandings, Constantine called together church leaders in Nicaea in AD 325 to write a creed that everybody could agree upon. Fifty-six years later the creed was slightly expanded. Since that time, Christians have looked to this creed as a great explanation of the basics of their faith.

EXAMINE THE CASE

The entire Nicene Creed is around 220 words long, and you can find it online. But in summary it says Christians believe in:

- one God the Father Almighty, maker of heaven and earth;
- one Lord Jesus Christ, the only begotten Son of God;
- the Holy Spirit, who proceeds from the heavenly Father;
- Jesus being made into man through the virgin Mary, suffering under Pontius Pilate, dying, being buried, and rising from the dead on the third day;
- Jesus coming again to judge all people and rule forever; and
- the importance of church and baptism.

The Boy Scout and Nicene creeds unify people. Creeds help us know how we should act and what we believe in. Many times in the early church the apostle Paul worked to unify God's body. He wrote to the Christians in Ephesus to be unified and bonded together through "one Lord, one faith, one baptism; one God and Father of all, who is over all and through all and in all" (Ephesians 4:5–6).

Sounds something like the Nicene Creed, huh? Find the Nicene Creed on your computer and see if you can memorize it. Then you'll be able to say it and shout, "I believe!"

FINAL WORD

"One Lord, one faith, one baptism; one God and Father of all, who is over all and through all and in all" *Ephesians 4:5–6*.

HISTORY THAT STANDS TALL

No tree stands taller than the coastal redwood. This majestic tree can grow more than 300 feet tall. In 2006 naturalists found one that rose over 379 feet—that's longer than a football field! Redwood trunks get so big around that you can build a tunnel and drive a car through them. At three places in northern California, tunnels have been made that allow cars to pass through a redwood. Not only do these trees grow to gigantic proportions, but they also live a long time. Scientists estimate redwoods can survive more than 2,000 years.

You'd think such a massive tree would have roots that plunge hundreds of feet into the ground. But just the opposite is true. Redwood roots go down only about four to six feet. The roots do, however, spread out more than 125 feet. By intertwining their roots with those of neighboring trees, redwoods strengthen and hold each other up.

EXAMINE THE CASE

When it comes to examining the validity of the Bible, it's important to look for corroborating evidence written by other historians. *Webster's* dictionary defines *corroborate* this way: "to make more certain; confirm." Several historians and other ancient writers did write about Jesus in a way that intertwines and strengthens the stories found in the Gospels.

Not only did Jewish historian Josephus and Tacitus (the most important Roman historian of the first century) write about Jesus' life, but Pliny the Younger, a governor in northwestern Turkey, and other Jewish and Roman writers also documented what Jesus did.

"The fact is that we have better historical documentation for Jesus than for the founder of any other ancient religion," says Bible scholar and professor Edwin Yamauchi. Even without the New Testament and other Christian writings, Yamauchi says other ancient non-Christian sources let us know that Jesus was a Jewish teacher; many people believed that he performed healings; some people believed he was the Messiah; he was rejected by the Jewish leaders; he was crucified under Pontius Pilate; despite this shameful death, his followers—who believed that he was still alive—spread beyond Palestine; and men and women, slave and free worshiped him as God.

All of this evidence helps us understand the real Jesus. It supports and confirms the kind, just God we read about in the Bible. And according to Jeremiah 9:24, that's something to boast about.

FINAL WORD

"Let the one who boasts boast about this: that they have the understanding to know me, that I am the Lord, who exercises kindness, justice and righteousness on earth" *Jeremiah 9:24*.

JARRING
TRUTHS

Crack! The shepherd boy startled at the sound. He didn't expect the stone that he'd aimlessly thrown into a cave to break anything. Curious, he searched the cave and made the greatest archaeological discovery of the twentieth century.

Okay, there are actually many stories about how the Dead Sea Scrolls were discovered in 1947. Some say Bedouin herders were searching the caves in Israel for a lost goat. Others claim they were looking for treasure when they came across nearly a dozen caves that contained large pottery jars with ancient scrolls inside. Or it could've been the shepherd boy who threw a rock and then told his tribe about what he'd found. Many mysteries still surround the Dead Sea Scrolls. But one thing is no mystery—these ancient documents contain the words of God.

More than 800 scrolls were found, written on parchment, papyrus, or leather. Some dated back more than 250 years before Jesus was born. They were so brittle that some scrolls took years to unroll. Others were in pieces and had to be put together like a puzzle. Biblical scholars joined archaeologists to piece the scrolls together. Soon they had identified sections of every Old Testament book of the Bible except for one.

Many of the books had multiple copies. Among the scrolls, parts of the Psalms were discovered thirty-nine times!

EXAMINE THE CASE

The Dead Sea Scrolls were an amazing discovery. But do you want to hear something even more amazing? When scholars compared the words on the scrolls with the same books in the Bible, they found that what we read has been transmitted with 99.99 percent accuracy. Many of the Dead Sea Scrolls were written a couple hundred years before Christ was born, yet his birth fulfilled many of the prophecies they contained.

At the beginning of one of Jesus' most famous sermons, he says, "Do not think that I have come to abolish the Law or the Prophets; I have not come to abolish them but to fulfill them" (Matthew 5:17). It's important for us to know what's written in the Old Testament. Jesus fulfills the promises God made to his people thousands of years ago. By reading the Old Testament, we gain a fuller understanding of God and his plan to save his people. Now that's the jarring truth.

FINAL WORD

"Do not think that I have come to abolish the Law or the Prophets; I have not come to abolish them but to fulfill them" *Matthew 5:17.*

DO THE GOOD THING

Joshua had recently prayed to ask Jesus to be his Savior and forgive his sins. When he heard about the church youth group, he figured it'd be a perfect way to grow in his new faith. Just one problem: the youth group usually started with some sort of competition. Dodgeball, kickball, capture the flag, duck-duck-goose—the game didn't matter, Josh was all about winning. Sometimes Josh's competitive juices took over, and he ended up cussing or pushing somebody. Every week he'd commit himself to not saying a bad word. Every game he'd fail.

Finally, the youth pastor pulled Joshua aside and encouraged him to change his motivation. Instead of trying *not* to sin by avoiding bad language or getting too physical, he encouraged Josh to focus on *doing* something positive during the game.

The following week Joshua decided he wanted to say three nice things to his teammates or opponents as they competed together. Not only did Josh's attitude and language improve, but the other kids also started to look forward to playing with him.

EXAMINE THE CASE

What changed? When Joshua first attended youth group, he focused on not breaking one of God's laws. But as followers of Christ, we should strive to live according to his rules. Do you see the difference? Many Christians put so much effort into avoiding sin that they live rule-bound, joyless lives. God doesn't want us focused on what not to do, but on what he wants us to do. Our actions should change not only us, but also the people around us. When the youth pastor told Joshua to aim at doing good, it changed everything.

In the book of Titus, the apostle Paul explains to his young friend why Jesus gave his life for us. Through Jesus' death, we're cleansed from sin and able to focus on doing good deeds (Titus 2:14). With Jesus in our lives, we're free from sin. The writers of the Bible used many different words to describe sin. The most frequently used one means "missing the mark." And we'll miss the mark if we focus on avoiding the bad things instead of doing good things. When we totally commit ourselves to doing good deeds and following God, we will live energized lives and avoid sin's trappings.

FINAL WORD

"He gave his life to free us from every kind of sin, to cleanse us, and to make us his very own people, totally committed to doing good deeds" *Titus 2:14 NLT.*

SCREEN-GLARING MISTAKE

How much time do you spend staring at a screen every day? It could be an iPad. Maybe it's the TV or computer. Other kids seem totally engrossed by their smartphone. Research shows that kids spend between five and seven hours each day looking at a screen. That's nearly fifty hours a week—more than a full-time job! Take away school and sleep and there isn't much time left for playing, talking with friends, eating, and having fun.

Wait! you say. *I have fun talking with my friends on Facebook and through text messages.* But face-to-face communication and communicating electronically are two very different things. A respected neuroscientist says hours of interacting on social networking sites may damage your brain. Research suggests that sites such as Facebook decrease attention spans, encourage instant gratification, and foster self-centeredness.

Watching other screens can have harmful side effects as well. Studies show that too much screen time can contribute to weight problems (because we're sitting, not moving around), make it harder to fall asleep (looking at a bright screen doesn't allow our brains to slow down and rest at night), and possibly lead to poor grades (a teacher's lecture can seem boring when there aren't explosions).

EXAMINE THE CASE

While the computer—and other screens—can make homework and communication easier, it shouldn't replace real-life relationships. Friendships and communication skills are best formed face-to-face. As Exodus 33:11 says, "The Lord would speak to Moses face to face, as one speaks to a friend."

God is a personal God. He spoke to Moses personally. As a boy Samuel heard God speak to him in the temple. And when God spoke to Paul, he became a champion for the faith and wrote much of the New Testament. God wants us to build relationships the same way that he does. Think of some ways you can connect with your friends in real life. Maybe you could do a scavenger hunt or play board games. The next time you get together with friends, try to avoid watching a movie or playing video games. Instead do something active where you can talk and get to know each other better. And personally, pick out a day this week when you try to avoid screens altogether. It won't be easy. But as you go through your day, every time you're tempted to look at a screen, thank God for loving you and being your Savior. As you pray to him, talk to God like you'd speak to a friend. He's a friend who will never let you down.

FINAL WORD

"The Lord would speak to Moses face to face, as one speaks to a friend" *Exodus 33:11*.

A MATTER OF BLACK AND WHITE

God created amazing colors. Think about a bright field of wildflowers or a stunning rainbow painted across a gray sky. But he also made some pretty cool things in black and white.

Zebras possess fantastic black and white stripes. Scientists have studied these animals and discovered their stripes may serve several purposes. In addition to making them look like referees at a basketball game, zebra stripes confuse horseflies. These blood-sucking pests are attracted to animals with dark coats. A zebra's coat reflects light in a way that doesn't appeal to the insect, so they leave them alone. In addition, researchers believe that a group of zebras may appear as one super-large animal to a predator. The stripes combine to create a visually imposing figure and scare away potential danger.

The yellow-lipped sea krait is a poisonous black-and-white snake that God gave a cool trait. It looks like it has two heads! Its head and its tail are nearly identical. So when the sea krait searches for food in coral reefs, at the same time it appears that its head is looking around for predators.

EXAMINE THE CASE

When it comes to following Christ, God made some things black and white—and for good reason. As a Christian, you must believe in God the Father, Jesus the Son, and the Holy Spirit. It's also a black-and-white fact that everybody falls short of God's perfect holiness. We all sin and need a Savior. That's where Jesus comes in. His perfect sacrifice makes it possible for us to know God personally.

In addition to these core beliefs, God has given us rules to follow. The Ten Commandments tell us to obey our parents, worship only God, and not to lie, steal, or kill. We're also instructed to help the poor, widows, and orphans. The Bible says to watch what you say, put others' needs ahead of your own, and honor your body. James 4:17 puts living for God in clear terms: "If anyone, then, knows the good they ought to do and doesn't do it, it is sin for them." When it comes to black-and-white rules, one of the most obvious is to stay away from sin. Write down one thing you know you should do but usually avoid:

• • •

Commit to doing it—and commit to staying away from sin.

FINAL WORD

"If anyone, then, knows the good they ought to do and doesn't do it, it is sin for them" *James 4:17.*

COPYCAT FAITH?

Ten cats were in a boat. One jumped out. How many were left?

None. They were copycats.

That's an old joke. The problem of being a copycat is nothing new. Nobody likes to be called a copycat, just like nobody wants to be copied. We want to be unique. We love to be creative with the way we look, the way we speak, and even the way we write.

In school, it's important to be unique in what we write, because if we copy somebody else's work we could get in trouble. The problem of plagiarism continues to increase in high schools and colleges. With so much information on the Internet, some students cut and paste their papers together instead of researching and writing things in their own words.

Plagiarism is obviously wrong. But in recent years, a popular book asserted that Christianity was plagiarized. The book was made into a movie in which one of the characters said, "Nothing in Christianity is original." The book (and movie) claims all of Christianity's core beliefs were copied from other religions and myths.

EXAMINE THE CASE

Instead of believing popular books and movies, we need to base our beliefs on hard evidence. Award-winning author and New Testament historian Michael Licona *has* studied the evidence. He speaks around the world and debates people who try to knock holes in Christianity. Licona has looked at the myths and religions, some of which started before Jesus came to earth. Writers have claimed the Persian god Mithras was born of a virgin; however, the myth says he was actually born from a rock. (Yes, a rock.) Solid scholarship conclusively shows that parallels between Christianity and other religions aren't accurate.

Then there's the biggest difference between Christianity and other religions: Jesus Christ. First John 4:9 tells us, "This is how God showed his love among us: He sent his one and only Son into the world that we might live through him." Jesus is the first, and only, God to sacrifice himself for your sins and rise from the dead. "The consensus among modern scholars— *nearly universal*—is that there were no dying and rising gods that preceded Christianity," Licona says. Don't be confused. Christianity isn't copied. Its core beliefs are original, unique, and true.

FINAL WORD

"This is how God showed his love among us: He sent his one and only Son into the world that we might live through him" *1 John 4:9.*

KEEP GOING AND GOING AND GOING

Have you ever visited the ocean? The constant crashing of the waves is awe-inspiring. The ocean continually moves. We see that movement as waves pound the beach. And although we can't see below the surface, the ocean actually moves faster at greater depths.

Can you think of other things that keep going and going and going? Write down a couple.

You might have written down *the wind*. Wind constantly blows near the ocean and at great heights in the atmosphere. The sun always shines. We may not see it if it's cloudy, but that doesn't mean the sun has stopped sending out heat and light. The earth also continually rotates and revolves. We may not feel it, but our world is spinning at more than 1,000 miles per hour, and we're orbiting around the sun at about 67,000 miles per hour. Time would've been another good answer. Time constantly moves forward, ticking second after second into the future.

EXAMINE THE CASE

God created many things to function constantly. And in 1 Thessalonians 5:16–18, the apostle Paul tells us three things we should always be doing: rejoicing, praying, and giving thanks.

Living out that command seems pretty impractical. Does God expect you to walk around constantly shouting, "Praise God! He is good! I thank God for all his blessings"? You could do that, but you might get some strange looks.

Instead, as followers of Jesus, we should look at these things like breathing. We don't have to think about breathing—it just happens naturally. Similarly, we should pray, praise, and thank God all the time. *Praying continually* doesn't mean you have to go around with your head bowed and eyes closed (that's just a good way to get a concussion). But we should be thinking about God all the time and have our thoughts focused on him. We also need to be always rejoicing. Maybe you feel like there's nothing to be happy about. School is hard. You sprained your ankle. You feel like your parents give your sister more attention. All of these circumstances are temporary (although they may not feel that way). Your relationship with Christ is eternal. No matter what's going on in your life, you can trust that God has a plan for you and will give you the strength to accomplish his will. And his love for you will keep going, and going, and going.

FINAL WORD

"Rejoice always, pray continually, give thanks in all circumstances; for this is God's will for you in Christ Jesus" *1 Thessalonians 5:16–18*.

LIFE-GIVING LIGHT

What's your favorite color? In a worldwide survey conducted in seventeen countries, the most popular color by far was ... blue. Four out of every ten people picked blue as their favorite color. Just 14 percent chose purple, which came in second. The least popular color was white, which ranked last in every country except Mexico, Brazil, and China. Blue is also the most popular color in nature. Seventy percent of the planet is covered in blue water—not to mention the blue sky that surrounds us.

> Light gives life to the natural world. Similarly, light gives life in our spiritual lives.

According to research, green is the second most common color in God's creation.

It may not be easy being green (at least for some frogs). But being green is important to plants. A plant's greenness keeps it alive. Chlorophyll, the pigment that makes plants green, helps the plant create food through photosynthesis. In photosynthesis, light energy is converted into chemical energy. Carbon dioxide, water, and sunlight combine in the process of photosynthesis to make glucose, which the plant stores as food.

EXAMINE THE CASE

Enough with the science lesson, you may be thinking. But without light, plants couldn't grow and life couldn't exist. Light gives life to the natural world. Similarly, light gives life in our spiritual lives. At the beginning of the Gospel of John, we read that Jesus "was life, and that life was the light of all mankind." God's Son gives us life. Without Jesus' light, we'd live in spiritual darkness.

In John 10:10 Jesus says, "I have come that they may have life, and have it to the full." Not only does Jesus give us life through our beating heart and ability to breathe in and out, but he also gives us an abundant life. God gives us a joy that people who don't know him can't understand. He gives us purpose and allows our lives to make a difference for him. Those who don't know Christ personally have no idea what it means to live life to its fullest. God gives our lives meaning, direction, and joy.

Take time today to thank Jesus for his life-giving light. Then spend a few minutes looking up these verses. Write down one key fact from each verse that you learn about the light:

John 9:5:

James 1:17:

2 Corinthians 4:6:

Make sure you're absorbing Jesus' life-giving light as much as possible.

FINAL WORD

"The thief comes only to steal and kill and destroy; I have come that they may have life, and have it to the full" *John 10:10.*

HELP OTHERS, HELP YOURSELF

Have you ever heard the saying, "God helps those who help themselves"? You won't find those words in the Bible. The phrase probably came from an ancient Greek fable called "Hercules and the Waggoner."

In the story, a man is driving a heavily loaded wagon across a muddy road. Suddenly, the wheels get stuck. No matter how hard the horses pull, the wagon won't budge. The waggoner looks to the sky and cries out for the mighty Hercules to help him. Hercules appears and says, "Put your shoulder to the wheel. The gods help them that help themselves." That saying may be true in Greek mythology and fables, but what does the one true God say?

Numerous times the Bible talks about helping *others*, not yourself. Philippians 2:3 says, "In humility value others above yourselves." First Peter 4:10 adds, "Each of you should use whatever gift you have received to serve others, as faithful stewards of God's grace in its various forms."

EXAMINE THE CASE

As you study Jesus' life, you'll discover that he was all about helping others. Dozens of times in the Gospels, Jesus demonstrated his healing powers. He healed the sick, crippled, blind, deaf, even the dead. And he helped people in many other ways, such as teaching them about God's grace and plan for their lives. When we take time to help somebody, we're following one of God's most precious commands.

Think of some ways you can help the people around you. Maybe you can pull a neighbor's weeds or shovel their driveway. Perhaps there's somebody you could tutor at school. You could even volunteer in the nursery at church. As you serve people, think of this acrostic:

Heaven's
Example
Loves
Perfectly

By helping others, you're following Jesus' example and demonstrating God's love. Not only that, but also God has wired you to enjoy helping. Serving makes you feel good and has physical advantages. Studies show that people who volunteer to help are healthier and make better choices in their lives. So benefit God, benefit society, benefit yourself, and get out there and serve. Then maybe you can help create a new popular saying: "God helps those who help others."

FINAL WORD

"Each of you should use whatever gift you have received to serve others, as faithful stewards of God's grace in its various forms" *1 Peter 4:10*.

DON'T BE
AT A LOSS

For more than 100 years, researchers have studied the effects of summer break on students. While summer means lots of fun, no homework, and few responsibilities, it also means learning loss. You actually lose ground academically. Lower-income students are hit the hardest, losing an average of two months of reading achievement during the summer. Many of these students have few books at home and aren't encouraged to read outside of school. As a result, by fifth grade some children are nearly three grade levels behind their peers in reading.

Research also shows all students typically score lower on standardized tests at the end of the summer than on the same test taken at the end of the school year. Math abilities decline as well. What's the solution? No more summer break?

Don't worry. Summer break isn't in jeopardy. The solution is actually quite simple: You must engage your brain. Just putting away video games, turning off the TV, and reading a book can make a huge difference. Play a strategy game with your family or a friend. Put together a puzzle. Your mind is like a muscle. You have to use it to strengthen it.

EXAMINE THE CASE

Learning loss doesn't only hinder your academic abilities. It can affect your walk with Christ. If you "take a break" from God, your relationship will suffer. On the other hand, by engaging with God through reading the Bible and going to church, you'll know what he expects and grow closer to him. In Joshua 1:8 the Israelite leader says, "Keep this Book of the Law always on your lips; meditate on it day and night, so that you may be careful to do everything written in it. Then you will be prosperous and successful." Joshua wanted God's people to talk about God's Word, think about God's Word, and follow God's Word. If they did that, the results would take care of themselves—the people would be prosperous and successful.

The same thing is true for you today. Make a plan to get into the Bible on a regular basis. Maybe you'll try to read the Bible in a year (there are lots of plans online). Perhaps you can begin a Bible study with your friends. When you keep learning about God, you'll never be at a loss.

FINAL WORD

"Keep this Book of the Law always on your lips; meditate on it day and night, so that you may be careful to do everything written in it. Then you will be prosperous and successful"
Joshua 1:8.

GOD'S BEST COMMERCIAL

Can you guess the most watched TV show ever in the United States? The answer is the Super Bowl.

Which one? you ask.

Super Bowls are old pros at setting records. Super Bowl XLIV (that's forty-four for you non-Romans) witnessed the New Orleans Saints defeating the Indianapolis Colts. The Saints not only won their first championship, but also helped break a record for most watched show—with 106.5 million viewers—that had stood since 1983 when 106 million people saw the final episode of *M.A.S.H.* (ask your parents about this popular TV show that ran from 1972 to 1983). The 2011 Super Bowl garnered 111 million viewers. And the 2012 Super Bowl did even better with 111.3 million people tuning in. The 2013 Super Bowl dropped down to 108 million viewers, but is still one of the all-time most seen shows.

While football's championship game can be exciting, a lot of people watch for the commercials. Advertisers often bring out their best and funniest commercials for the Super Bowl. And they'd better, because it costs big money to appear during the big game. For a thirty-second spot during the 2012 Super Bowl, companies paid $3.5 million! Of course, advertisers know what they're doing. During many shows, the commercials get skipped or muted. But fans actually turn up their sets to see Super Bowl advertisements.

EXAMINE THE CASE

Companies know the power of a good ad. During a 2012 playoff game between the Denver Broncos and New England Patriots, the Christian ministry Focus on the Family paid for a commercial that featured children reciting John 3:16. Millions watched as kids told them God loved them so much that he sent his only Son to die so they could have eternal life.

Commercials to promote Christianity aren't limited to TV screens. You are God's best commercial. Second Corinthians 5:20 says, "We are therefore Christ's ambassadors, as though God were making his appeal through us." God wants us to be a walking commercial for him. Commercials effectively tell a message in a little bit of time. We should do the same.

Think about your words and actions in the last week. When people spent time with you, what message did they receive? Were you kind? Did you put others' needs above your own? As you live your life for Jesus, remember that people are watching to see what it means to be a Christian. So always be thinking: *What can I do to be a powerful walking commercial for God?*

FINAL WORD

"We are therefore Christ's ambassadors, as though God were making his appeal through us. We implore you on Christ's behalf: Be reconciled to God" *2 Corinthians 5:20.*

OLDIE BUT A GOODIE

What would you rather have: a brand-new bike or a rusty old one? A new one, right? But sometimes new isn't better. Old things can be valuable.

In 2010 a man went to a garage sale and paid $5 for a child's sketch of a man's face on a bright orange-and-yellow-checked background. It turned out the sketch was drawn by a famous artist when he was ten years old—and could be worth $2 million! In 2012 a man in Ohio purchased a poster advertising a Pablo Picasso art exhibit for $14.14. Months later he sold it for $7,000 after he discovered the poster was drawn by the artist himself. Countless stories exist of people finding an old piece of junk and learning it's a precious antique.

EXAMINE THE CASE

While new translations of the Bible come out all the time, the oldest books of the Bible were written 1,500 years *before* Jesus was born. That's old. Advertisers love to bombard us with messages about products being "new and improved" or having a "new advanced formula." But when it comes to the Bible, you can't improve something that's already perfect.

After Jesus died, a lot of stories circulated about his life. Some followed the facts. Others were made up. The early church studied the writings about Jesus and only included the oldest and most accurate ones in the Bible. About 400 years after Jesus' birth, the twenty-seven-book New Testament was first put together.

Today, some scholars like to grab headlines by saying *new* books should be put in the Bible. If it's new, it's news, so they'll claim anything to make a splash. They dig up stories that make wild claims about Jesus. These scholars often end up on TV and their opinions confuse people or make them feel the Bible is incomplete. When you hear outrageous stories about Jesus or reports of "new" gospels, you can be confident that the traditional books in the Bible are the ones God wanted. Your Bible tells the complete story. It doesn't change. It doesn't fade. And it won't go away.

The Bible is an oldie and a goodie. It's valuable. And when it comes to old, rusty bikes, don't dismiss them so soon. Some collectible ones are worth thousands of dollars.

FINAL WORD

"Your word, Lord, is eternal; it stands firm in the heavens" *Psalm 119:89*.

IT'S IN
THE BLOOD

Have you ever heard the saying, "Blood is thicker than water"? Basically, it means the bonds between family members are stronger than the relationships between friends. That may be true, but it's definitely true that blood *is* thicker than water—twice as thick, because of all the cells, nutrients, gases, and proteins it contains. Blood makes up about 10 percent of your body weight and is key to sustaining your life. Red blood cells carry oxygen around your body. Their unique shape (sort of like a dented Life Savers mint) allows them to twist and travel through the tiniest blood vessels. It takes less than a minute for a single red blood cell to make the journey away from and back to your heart. That trip causes a lot of wear and tear. Your body constantly makes new red blood cells, because these cells only last about four months before they have to be replaced.

Just like blood is crucial to physical life, it's also vital to your spiritual life. Hebrews 9:22 says, "The law requires that nearly everything be cleansed with blood, and without the shedding of blood there is no forgiveness."

EXAMINE THE CASE

If you read the first five books of the Bible, you'll find several hundred references to animal sacrifices and offerings. That can sound kind of gruesome. But according to God's law, sin comes with a horrible price. The basic concept God wanted to teach his people is that sin comes with the penalty of death (Romans 3:23). When Adam and Eve committed the original sin of eating from the tree of the knowledge of good and evil, God warned that the result would be death (Genesis 2:17). Sin is rebelling against God. When we're in rebellion, we can't be close to a perfectly holy God. To restore that relationship, God requires the shedding of blood (Hebrews 9:22).

But, you may say, *we don't sacrifice animals today.* You're right. That's because Jesus came to earth.

Some people will try to tell you God is cruel because he sent his Son, knowing he'd suffer and die. But instead of demonstrating cruelty, it actually shows God's love for all people. He sent his Son to pay a debt that we could never repay. Only one sacrifice was pure and perfect enough to cover all the sins of the world. Jesus willingly shed his blood, suffered, died, and rose again to save us. It was the ultimate act of love.

Think of ways you can show your love for God. Write some down:

_____

_____

Live in a way that shows God how grateful you are for his sacrifice, and thank him for shedding his blood.

FINAL WORD

"Jesus Christ, who is the faithful witness, the firstborn from the dead, and the ruler of the kings of the earth. To him who loves us and has freed us from our sins by his blood" *Revelation 1:5*.

PRINTS AMONG MEN

Nobody else in the world has fingerprints like yours. That's a fact that should make you feel special and make crime fighters feel confident. Since 1910, fingerprint evidence has been used to identify and convict criminals. Your fingerprints actually start forming six months *before* you're born. Even identical twins have unique fingerprints.

Take a few minutes to examine your fingerprints. All you need is a stamp pad and piece of paper. Carefully roll one of your fingertips on the inkpad. Then roll that same finger onto the paper. You may need to try it a few times to get a clean print. Experts have identified seven common patterns of fingerprints—the arch, loop, double loop, pocked loop, mixed, tentarch, and whorl. You can look up the different patterns on the Internet. To an untrained eye, fingerprints can appear fairly similar. But once you know what to look for, the differences pop off the page. If your family is willing, take their fingerprints as well. Grab a magnifying glass to examine them more closely. Notice how each one is unique.

EXAMINE THE CASE

When Jesus came to earth, he left a lot of evidence about his true identity. We might not have his actual fingerprints, but we have plenty of "prophetic fingerprints" to prove Jesus was God's promised Messiah. The word *Messiah* means "anointed one." In the Old Testament, God promised his people to send a Messiah to deliver them from their oppression. Many prophets wrote about different characteristics and details that the Messiah would possess. In one of the most famous passages of Scripture, Isaiah 53, the prophet wrote that he would be "rejected by mankind," "[take] up our sorrows," be "pierced for our transgressions," be "led like a lamb to the slaughter," "[bear] the sin of many," and "[make] intercession for the transgressors." There are many other details in that passage, but can you think of anyone who fits that description?

Early in the book of Acts, Peter said, "But the things which God announced beforehand by the mouth of all the prophets, that His Christ would suffer, He has thus fulfilled" (Acts 3:18 NASB). Jesus fulfilled prophecies written hundreds of years before his birth. In fact, Jesus is the sole individual in all of history who has matched the prophetic fingerprint of God's anointed one.

FINAL WORD

"The precious blood of Christ, the sinless, spotless Lamb of God. God chose him as your ransom long before the world began, but he has now revealed him to you in these last days" *1 Peter 1:19–20 NLT*.

CHANGE YOUR MIND

Some historians consider Albert Einstein the greatest scientist who ever lived. Often called the "father of modern physics," Einstein didn't amaze his teachers early in life. He struggled with talking until he was nine, causing some of his teachers to wonder if he was mentally challenged. Despite his limited speaking abilities, Einstein had an inquisitive mind and was drawn to math. By age twelve, he excelled in geometry. By sixteen, he'd mastered calculus. It was also at age sixteen that Einstein wondered what it'd be like to ride his bike on a beam of light. Over the next sixty years, Einstein helped prove the existence of molecules, explained the nature of space and time, and changed the way that scientists studied light.

Einstein may be famous for his scientific achievements, but he's equally known for his insightful sayings. He once defined *insanity* as "doing the same thing over and over again and expecting different results."

If we honestly look at our lives, we'll have to admit that we often live *insanely*. We want to get better grades at school, but we don't change our study habits. We hope to improve our trumpet playing, but we keep practicing the same way.

We desire to grow closer to God, but our Bibles remain on the shelf and we say the same prayers over and over.

EXAMINE THE CASE

Change isn't always easy, but it can be good. God is a God of newness. He wants us to think creatively and see life in fresh ways. He doesn't want us to act insane. Romans 12:2 says, "Do not conform to the pattern of this world, but be transformed by the renewing of your mind. Then you will be able to test and approve what God's will is." God gave us amazing minds that can solve problems, dream big dreams, and seek God's will. But we can't do any of that if we conform to this world.

As you build your life on Christ, seek to change your mind to be more like God's. If you feel like you're stuck in a cycle of insanity, break away! Turn off inappropriate TV shows. Stay away from harmful websites and YouTube videos. Switch up your music playlist. Renew your mind by focusing on God's truth and jumping into his Word. You may see life in a whole new way.

FINAL WORD

"Do not conform to the pattern of this world, but be transformed by the renewing of your mind. Then you will be able to test and approve what God's will is—his good, pleasing and perfect will" *Romans 12:2*.

ANGELS WE HAVE HEARD ON HIGH

We sing about them at Christmas and hang them on our tree, but how much do we really know about angels? Some people picture angels sitting on clouds and strumming harps. Others believe humans become angels when we die. But the Bible paints a very different picture. Angels are powerful God-created beings who existed before humankind. They worship God, protect his followers, and do the Father's will.

Look up these verses in the Bible and write down what you learn about angels:

Hebrews 1:14:

Matthew 4:10–11:

Psalm 91:11:

Revelation 5:11–12:

2 Kings 19:32–35:

Hebrews 13:2:

Luke 15:10:

Angels have played a huge role in the history of the world and had a part in many Bible stories. An angel shut the lions' mouths for Daniel (Daniel 6:22) and led the Israelites out of Egypt (Exodus 14:19). Angels also announced the birth of Jesus Christ.

EXAMINE THE CASE

It must be scary to meet an angel. Almost every time they appear, they say, "Don't be afraid." That's exactly what the angel Gabriel said to Mary. In Luke 1:30–32 Gabriel says, "Do not be afraid, Mary; you have found favor with God. You will conceive and give birth to a son, and you are to call him Jesus. He will be great and will be called the Son of the Most High." Angels were intimately involved with Jesus and his ministry during his entire time on earth. Angels told the shepherds about Jesus (Luke 2:8–15). Angels attended to Jesus' needs after he spent forty days in the desert. And when Jesus was arrested in the Garden of Gethsemane, he went willingly—even though he told Peter that he could call down more than twelve legions of angels (Matthew 26:53). If one angel can take care of 185,000 soldiers, just imagine what 72,000 angels could do!

Angels are amazing. As you learn more about Jesus and his angels, you'll discover angels are nothing to fear or worship (sadly, some people do worship angels). We should, however, emulate angels when it comes to worshiping God and protecting each other.

FINAL WORD

"Praise the Lord from the heavens; praise him in the heights above. Praise him, all his angels; praise him, all his heavenly hosts" *Psalm 148:1–2*.

TWISTED TONGUE

Do you have a favorite tongue twister? Some certainly are hard to say.

She sells seashells by the seashore can slide nimbly from your tongue. But to say *A tutor who tooted a flute tried to tutor two tooters to toot. Said the two to their tutor, "Is it harder to toot or to tutor two tooters to toot?"* can create quite a mess.

According to *Guinness World Records*, the most difficult tongue twister to say in the English language is, *The sixth sick sheikh's sixth sheep's sick.* (What does that even mean?) Try to say any of the above tongue twisters five times really fast. You'll probably mess up.

And that's not the only time our tongues mess up. We make mistakes with what we say every day. A cruel word slips out. We make fun of somebody's clothes. Our twisted tongues have power, because words have power. That's why Jesus' brother James warns us in James 3:6, "The tongue also is a fire, a world of evil among the parts of the body. It corrupts the whole body."

It's amazing to think that such a small part of the body is so powerful. The world's longest tongue measured less than four inches, yet the human tongue has ruined friendships,

started wars, and brought down nations. That's why as followers of Christ we should strive to tame our tongues and
watch what we say.

EXAMINE THE CASE

When it comes to speaking with power, nobody's words accomplish more than God's. The beginning of the Bible details how
God spoke everything into existence. Genesis 1:3 tells us, "God
said, 'Let there be light,' and there was light." God's words
made everything in the universe. Psalm 33:6 puts it this way:
"By the word of the Lord the heavens were made, their starry
host by the breath of his mouth."

But when you think about God's spoken word, you also have
to consider God's Word—Jesus. John 1:1 says, "In the beginning
was the Word, and the Word was with God, and the Word was
God." God's Son was with God in the beginning and through
him everything was made. Jesus is called "the Word," because
he proceeded from God to accomplish the Father's will on earth.
Jesus was more than a good teacher or healer (as some people
might want to tell you). He was the divine Word of God.

Words have a way of deeply impacting you and sinking into
your soul. That's exactly what Jesus wants to do in your life.
Embrace the Word of God and you'll discover the true power
of words.

FINAL WORD

"God said, 'Let there be light,' and there was light" *Genesis 1:3*.

SWEET AND SALTY

Marshmallows are amazing. Don't believe it? Just try these two experiments (but get a parent's permission first).

First, put two marshmallows on a paper plate. Place them in the microwave and cook on high for thirty seconds. They'll blow up nearly four times their original size! Carefully remove the marshmallows from the microwave and let them cool on the counter. Eat one of the marshmallows. Is it soft and gooey or hard and crunchy? If you cook it too long, it'll end up black on the inside. Put the other marshmallow back in the microwave for fifteen seconds. Allow it to shrink down and then form it into a funny shape. It'll eventually harden and stay that way.

For the other experiment, get a new marshmallow and pull it apart. The center of the marshmallow should feel sticky. Now dip one half into some water. What happens? The marshmallow is no longer sticky.

EXAMINE THE CASE

As God's children, we should stick close to him. But instead of stickiness, Jesus warns us about losing our "saltiness." In Mark 9:50 he says, "If [salt] loses its flavor, how do you make it salty again? You must have the qualities of salt among yourselves and live in peace with each other" (NLT).

For thousands of years, salt has been used to flavor and preserve foods. The Old Testament book of Ezekiel talks about newborn babies being rubbed with salt because of its purifying qualities. Later in the Bible, Jesus calls his followers "the salt of the earth." As Christians, we need to preserve his commands and keep ourselves pure. We should live with "saltiness" toward each other, encouraging fellow believers to stand strong for God. When people come in contact with us, we should "taste" different. Just like eating salty chips makes us thirsty, when people meet us they should become thirsty for Christ.

Think of ways you can stay salty. Certainly, reading your Bible is important; so is admitting your sins to Christ and praying for forgiveness. Then you need to commit to living out your Christian beliefs in the way you speak, the way you treat others, and what you feed your mind. Being sweet is nice; being salty is even better.

FINAL WORD

"Salt is good for seasoning. But if it loses its flavor, how do you make it salty again? You must have the qualities of salt among yourselves and live in peace with each other" *Mark 9:50 NLT.*

A HORSE, OF COURSE

Horses have always had a special relationship with humans. Some historians argue that the horse has helped humanity more than any other animal. Over thousands of years, horses have been used to quickly get from one place to another, plow a field, ride into battle, deliver information, compete for sport, provide therapy for people with certain disabilities, and pull wagons. People have eaten horse meat, drank horse milk, and tanned horse skins for leather.

Nobody can deny that horses are one of God's most amazing and helpful animals. Gallop through these horse facts:

Matthew Kowalski/Getty Images

- According to *Guinness World Records*, Big Jake is the world's biggest horse. This seven-foot-tall Belgian lives in Wisconsin.
- Horses have bigger eyes than any other mammal that lives on land.
- Horses sleep only three or four hours a day and do it standing up or lying down.
- Einstein, the world's smallest stallion, is only twenty inches tall.

- Horses drink around twelve gallons of water a day, but are capable of drinking more than twenty-five gallons.
- Horses can run up to forty-five miles per hour.

It's not horsing around to say horses have played a big role in his-

EXAMINE THE CASE

tory, including in the Bible. More than 175 verses mention horses. One of the best known can be found in Revelation 19:11, which describes Jesus Christ's second coming back to earth: "I saw heaven standing open and there before me was a white horse, whose rider is called Faithful and True." The color of Jesus' horse represents purity. His victory is assured. His entry triumphal.

And if you read a few verses later, you'll find that God's army rides just behind Jesus on their own white horses. Just imagine the picture of Jesus and his army riding from the heavens to victoriously reclaim the earth. Jesus knows the future. He wins. Anybody and anything that opposes God will be defeated.

Sometimes when you look at your future, you may get discouraged. You might not be able to see God's plan when difficult situations and circumstances get in the way. Before you give up hope, remember that Jesus knows your future and what role you'll play in his story. Ask Jesus to guide you according to his will, and then be willing to be led—just as a horse trusts its master.

FINAL WORD

"I saw heaven standing open and there before me was a white horse, whose rider is called Faithful and True. With justice he judges and wages war" *Revelation 19:11.*

SOURCES

Hot Dog Faith

15: "Paste-like and batter-like ...": Katherine Harmon, "What's in Your Wiener? Hot Dog Ingredients Explained," *Scientific American* blog, July 2, 2011, http://blogs.scientificamerican.com/observations/2011/07/02/whats-in-your-wiener-hot-dog-ingredients-explained/.

Dig In

18: "The Bible deserves ...": Daniel B. Wallace, quoted in Lee Strobel, *The Case for the Real Jesus* (Grand Rapids: Zondervan, 2007), 78.

Get the Message?

20: "The quantity and quality ...": Wallace, quoted in Strobel, *Case for the Real Jesus*, 83.

Eyewitness Account

28: "You're going to have to answer ...": Wallace story, quoted in Strobel, *Case for the Real Jesus*, 79.

More Than a Friend

30: "First, we have to quit ...": Wallace, quoted in Strobel, *Case for the Real Jesus*, 98.

Held Together

37: "How crazy is that ...": "Louie Giglio—

Laminin," June 6, 2008, http://www.youtube.com/
watch?v=F0-NPPIeeRk.

Reality Check

44: "I can't stress this enough ...": Paul Copan, quoted in
Strobel, *Case for the Real Jesus*, 243.

Heart of the Matter

46: "So the core message ...": Craig A. Evans, quoted in
Strobel, *Case for the Real Jesus*, 35.

No Bones about It

50: "The possibility of it ...": Amos Kloner, quoted in Strobel, *Case for the Real Jesus*, 148.

Rewards of Patience

55: Marshmallow study: "The Marshmallow Study Revis-
ited," University of Rochester (N.Y.), October 11, 2012,
http://www.rochester.edu/news/show.php?id=4622.

Alive and Awesome

65: "Hey! Can you keep it down?": Jocelyn S., "Safe in an
Earthquake," *Clubhouse* magazine, April 2011, p. 3.

Get Out of Your Head

72: "In many cases—not all ...": Michael Licona, quoted in
Strobel, *Case for the Real Jesus*, 136.

Coming Through Loud and Clear

80: "Unlike the telephone game ...": Craig A. Evans, quoted
in Strobel, *Case for the Real Jesus*, 58.

A Good Memory

82: "Rabbis became famous ...": Craig Blomberg, quoted in

Lee Strobel, *The Case for Christ* (Grand Rapids: Zondervan, 1998), 43.

Truth Wins

96: "Even though the Internet …": Edwin Yamauchi, quoted in Strobel, *Case for the Real Jesus*, 184–85.

Going Worldwide

102: "In addition to Greek manuscripts …": Bruce Metzger, quoted in Strobel, *Case for Christ*, 59.

Original Superhero

108: "He's no less than …": Paul Copan, quoted in Strobel, *Case for the Real Jesus*, 259–60.

Source of Confidence

114: "Matthew published his own …": Irenaeus, quoted in Strobel, *Case for Christ*, 24.

Most Embarrassing Moment

116: "Here's the point …": Craig Blomberg, quoted in Strobel, *Case for Christ*, 50.

Humble Hero

117: "The whole organization …": Mariano Rivera, quoted in Bryan Llenas, "Mariano Rivera Gets 602 to Become All-Time Saves Leader," *Fox New Latino*, September 19, 2011, http://latino.foxnews.com/latino/sports/2011/09/19/mariano-rivera-gets-number–602-to-become-all-time-saves-leader/.

117: "Yes, it does.…": Mariano Rivera, on *The Michael Kay Show*, ESPN New York (1050 AM) podcast, September 16, 2011, http://espn.go.com/new-york/radio/archive?id=2693958.

SOURCES

Helping Others, Helping Christ

121: Piper Hayward story: Piper Hayward, "Water Girl," *Clubhouse* magazine, March 2013, pp. 22–23.

Can You Dig It?

124: "Archaeology has not …": John McRay, quoted in Strobel, *Case for Christ*, 100.

God Rules

127: Laws: http://realstrangelaws.com.

Act Like a Dog

130: "To have a relationship …": Gregory Boyd, quoted in Strobel, *Case for Christ*, 126.

The Secret to Giving

131: "Part of my daily …": Larry Stewart, quoted in Nanci Hellmich, "Santa Shares His Secret," *USA Today*, December 21, 2006, http://usatoday30.usatoday.com/news/nation/2006-12-20-santa-secret_x.htm.

Getting Stronger … by Resting

147: "Just due to the type …": Shane Hamman, quoted in Jesse Florea, "Shane Hamman: In God's Strength," *Clubhouse* magazine, June 2004, p. 22.

Better Than Gold

154: "Basically, the early church …": Bruce Metzger, quoted in Strobel, *Case for Christ*, 66.

History That Stands Tall

158: "The fact is …": Edwin Yamauchi, quoted in Strobel, *Case for Christ*, 86–87.

SOURCES

Copycat Faith?

168: "The consensus among ...": Michael Licona, quoted in Strobel, *Case for the Real Jesus*, 160; Licona is quoting T. N. D. Mettinger's book *The Riddle of Resurrection* (Coronet Books, 2001).

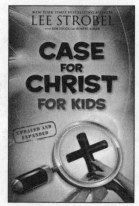